GHOSTS *of*
MISSISSIPPI'S
GOLDEN TRIANGLE

ALAN BROWN

Haunted
America

Published by Haunted America
A Division of The History Press
Charleston, SC
www.historypress.net

First published 2016

ISBN 978-1-5316-9996-3

Library of Congress Control Number: 2016936702

To Kenny and Andrea Reynolds, who have close ties to Columbus.

CONTENTS

CONTENTS

ACKNOWLEDGEMENTS

A number of people assisted me with this project. My son-in-law, Kenny Reynolds, and his mother, Gail, provided me with the photographs of the Hollyhocks Gift Shop. Mona Vance, librarian at the Columbus Public Library, was very helpful in my efforts to find historic information about the sites in the book. I am also indebted to the homeowners who graciously shared their ghost stories with me during the Pilgrimage of Homes. Lonnie C's Halloween broadcast of his investigation of the Gulf Ordnance Munitions Plant was extremely helpful. Beth Nil's and Terry Sweeney's contributions to the Gulf Ordnance Munitions Plant chapter are also greatly appreciated. My colleague Elizabeth Threatt and her husband, Patrick Threatt, assisted me with collecting information and photographs relating to Mississippi State University. Another colleague, Mitzi Green, told me about one of Columbus's lesser-known ghost stories: the haunting of the Hollyhocks Gift Shop. My friend Greg Jones gave me invaluable advice regarding the photographs. Bruce Shulze helped me locate the Library of Congress photographs that appear in the "Waverly" chapter. However, this book would probably never have been published without the persistence of my editor, Candice Lawrence, who never lost faith in the project—or in me. Of course, my greatest supporter is my wife, Marilyn, who accompanied me on my travels and assisted me with locating and photographing most of the buildings featured in *Ghosts of Mississippi's Golden Triangle.*

Introduction

L ocated in the eastern-central portion of Mississippi, the Golden Triangle is formed by the cities of Columbus, Starkville and West Point, as well as Lowndes, Oktibbeha and Clay Counties. The region was given the name "the Golden Triangle" to encourage the economic development of the three cities, all of which owed their prosperity to the rich black soil of the Black Belt. The production of cotton made this region one of the wealthiest in the entire state in the nineteenth century.

The history of Mississippi's Golden Triangle can be traced all the way back to the earliest European exploration of the South. In 1540, Hernando de Soto forded the Tombigbee River and passed through what is now Columbus in his search for the fabled city of Eldorado. One of the first white residents of the area, John Pitchlynnn, established a farm on Plymouth Bluff. His property became an important stronghold on the Choctaw frontier during the Creek War of 1813–14. Following the signing of the Treaty of the Choctaws in 1816, the Choctaws ceded ten thousand acres of land east of the Tombigbee River in exchange for $6,000 per year for twenty years.

In 1817, the first settler, Thomas Thomas, erected a log cabin in the Columbus area and became the town's first settler. "Possum Town," as it was called by the Choctaws, grew steadily. It was officially chartered as a town on February 10, 1821, by the Mississippi state legislature. Franklin School, the first public school in Mississippi, was founded in Columbus that same year. During the Civil War, Columbus was protected from invasion by Federal forces, led by General Nathan Bedford Forrest, whose army was operating north of Columbus. Consequently, Columbus has one of the largest collections of antebellum homes in Mississippi, second only to Natchez. Following the Battle of Shiloh, Columbus became a hospital town, and many of its palatial homes became field hospitals.

Columbus gained national recognition after the Civil War when a group of ladies met in Twelve Gables and decided to place flowers on the graves of both Union and Confederate soldiers in Friendship Cemetery. When the ladies' generous act was reported in an article in the *New York Times*, Francis Miles Finch commemorated the event in his poem "The Blue and the Grey." This local observance of the debt paid by the nation's soldiers evolved into Memorial Day.

The archaeological record indicates that human beings have inhabited the Starkville area for more than 2,100 years. Much of this evidence is in the form of pottery shards and artwork discovered at the Herman Mound and Village site east of Starkville. Around the time of the Revolutionary War, the Choccuma tribe lived here until it was decimated by the Choctaw and Chickasaw Indians. White settlers began moving into the Starkville area following the signing of the Treaty of Dancing Rabbit, which ceded all of the Choctaw lands in Oktibbhea County. People looking for a good place to live built their homes around the area's two large springs. Three water mills were constructed on the Noxubee River. Because of the lumber mill, which supplied clapboards for houses in the area, Starkville became known as Boardtown. In 1835, Boardtown was renamed Starkville in honor of Revolutionary War hero General John Stark. That same year, Starkville became the county seat of Oktibbhea County. A one-room log structure served as Starkville's first courthouse and jail. Before 1861, the Starkville area consisted of small farms and a few large plantations. According to the 1860 census, 12,977 of Starkville's citizens were white; 7,631 were slaves.

The first Europeans to reach the West Point area were probably members of Hernando de Soto's expedition; it's believed they camped out here during the cold winter of 1541. However, thousands of years before de Soto's arrival, the Clay County area was populated primarily by horses, which freely roamed the grasslands before mysteriously disappearing. Later, the Chickasaws developed their own breed of horses. The French and English traders most likely came to this area in the 1690s. Following the Chickasaw removal in the 1830s, a number of plantations sprang up in Clay County, the most famous of which is Waverly, located ten miles east of West Point. Many of these magnificent homes are listed in the National Register of Historic Places. One of the state's most significant

Civil War battles was the Battle of West Point, during which General Nathan Bedford Forrest defeated an army three times the size of his force and halted General William Tecumseh Sherman's drive into Alabama. The Confederates suffered 144 casualties; the Union army lost 324 men.

Up until the twentieth century, the economy of the Golden Triangle was based largely on cotton production. Manufacturing replaced agriculture as the primary source of income for the population until the 1990s, when many industrial jobs were lost to restructuring. Today, the Golden Triangle is known for its educational institutions: the Mississippi University for Women and Mississippi State University. As the people of the Golden Triangle move into the future, they also look back to their past to remember their roots. Columbus's annual Pilgrimage of Homes, held each April, attracts thousands of people eager to catch a glimpse of the lives of the town's most privileged citizens in the nineteenth century. The Golden Triangle's storied past has also generated a large body of ghost lore, most of which centers on the fine old antebellum mansions that have survived the elements and the passage of time. These tales humanize the faces on the old portraits and faded photographs hanging on the walls in many of these old homes. Through the ghost stories of the Golden Triangle, we learn of the inhabitants' little triumphs and tragedies, which have become an indelible part of the region's oral history.

ABERDEEN

THE GREGG-HAMILTON HOUSE

The Gregg-Hamilton House was built on Commerce Street in 1950. The history of the Gregg-Hamilton House is inextricably connected to the Civil War. In 1864, Confederate general John Gregg was killed in the defense of Richmond, Virginia. His widow, Mary Frances "Molly" Garth Gregg, traveled to Virginia to retrieve her husband's corpse. She buried General Gregg's remains in the Odd Fellows Rest Cemetery in Aberdeen, where her father owned large tracts of land. Molly was so attached to her husband that she purchased the Gregg-Hamilton House so she could make frequent visits to his grave.

Over one hundred years later, the house was bought and restored by author Dr. Charles Hamilton. He was born in Pennsylvania in 1905 and raised in Kentucky. At the age of twenty-three, Dr. Hamilton moved to Mississippi. He was a professor of Christian education at Okolona College in Okolona, Mississippi. Dr. Hamilton served as rector of St. John's Episcopal Church in Aberdeen until 1942. His life-long interest in politics led him to serve in the state legislature from 1940 to 1944. Dr. Hamilton achieved literary fame as a regional writer who penned poetry—including the poems "Mississippi I Love You," "You Can't Steal First Base" and "The Flag Was Flame"—and books about the Civil War while living at the Gregg-Hamilton House in the 1940s.

In later years, the Gregg-Hamilton House became rental property and was divided into three units. Before long, people who lived there began sharing stories about strange activities inside the old house. One of these renters was Rayburn Reeves, who had not been told that the house was haunted before moving in. One night, Reeves and his wife heard a man and a woman arguing in the house. Fearing that the domestic disturbance might escalate into violence, Reeves went downstairs to investigate. He was puzzled when he discovered that he and his wife were the only ones living in the house at the time. Over time, the Reeveses began hearing strange sounds inside the house. Sometimes, after hearing the noises in a specific room, they smelled the scent of lavender in the room. Reeves and his wife eventually became used to living with a ghost in their house. However, not everyone who stayed in the house felt the same way. Reeves's mother was so frightened by the sound of the ghostly footsteps that she refused to return to the house for a long time. The strangest part of the house was an upstairs room where Reeves occasionally walked into cold spots.

Harold and Madies Conner rented an apartment in the Gregg-Hamilton House as well. Although they had a number of strange experiences while living there, one particular event stands out. At the time, no one lived upstairs; Cary and Patsy Claxton lived downstairs. One night, Madies was all alone in the apartment. Standing in a particular spot under the ceiling, she could hear a person walk eight feet in one direction and eight feet in the opposite direction above her. Madies called her mother but was told she was imagining things. She thought about calling the police but changed her mind when she considered the possibility that the officers would find nothing out of the ordinary when they arrived. Overcome with fear, she turned on the radio to drown out the noise, but she could still hear the footsteps walking back and forth. After what seemed an eternity, she heard Cary Claxton return home. She ran to the next-door apartment and begged him to go upstairs with her. Armed with nothing more than a flashlight, Cary walked through all of the upstairs rooms but neither saw nor heard anybody. The pacing ceased while Cary was upstairs, but after he went home, it started up again. Madies felt as if an invisible force were drawing her to that same spot under the ceiling. This turned out to be one of the longest nights of her life.

Unknown to Madies, Patsy Claxton had her own paranormal experiences in the house. She, too, had heard someone—or something—walking up the stairs. Even her Siamese cat sensed that there was something not quite "right" about the house. He refused to walk into one of the rooms. He would go up to the doorway and stop, raise his back and bristle. After a few seconds, the feline would run away and look back at something that no one else could see.

One of the owners of the house, Mary Elizabeth Hamilton, had heard the ghost stories before she and her husband moved in, but they never experienced anything out of the ordinary while they lived there. However, she began to place more credence in the tales one evening when a neighbor who had too many people staying in her house asked Mrs. Hamilton if a young married couple could spend a few days in the Gregg-Hamilton House. The next morning, the couple packed up and left because they had heard somebody walking around their room all night.

Another mysterious room in the Gregg-Hamilton House is the basement, which is called "the prison cell" because of the bars. Legend has it that Union soldiers were held prisoner there during the Civil War. Could it be that the unquiet spirts of these men are still unable to leave the place where they were held against their will?

ARTESIA

THE ARTESIA LIGHT

The history of Artesia is inextricably linked to the railroad. Artesia Junction, as it was originally known because of the large number of artesian wells in the area, came into being in the 1850s, when Columbus and Aberdeen refused to allow the Mobile & Ohio (M&O) Railroad to route through town because of all the smoke and noise. However, the M&O did extend a spur line to serve Columbus. The spur line joined the main line at what is now Artesia because the local planters gave the right of way to any railroad interested in passing through this part of Lowndes County.

The main line was completed around 1858–59, and Artesia Junction became a true railroad town. Travelers from all over the South spent the night at the Childsey House, a railroad-owned hotel. The hotel was renowned for its splendid meals. Guests dined on produce from St. Louis and fish from Mobile, all of which was brought to the town by the M&O Railroad. Twenty-five years after the Childsey House opened, it burned down and was never rebuilt. Artesia's boomtown days are long gone now. Today, the quaint little town of 440 people (as of the 2010 United States census) is a remnant of those long-ago days when people living in the rural South were dependent on the railroad.

Like many old railroad towns, Artesia has a railroad ghost. Legend has it that around the turn of the century, an elderly African American railroad watchman was walking the tracks between Artesia and Mayhew at about midnight when he was struck by a speeding train. Many people living in the region believe that if they stand by the tracks at midnight and are quiet, they can see the ghostly watchman swinging his glowing lantern as he makes his nightly rounds. For years, adventurous students from Mississippi State University parked on one of the bridges near the tracks and waited for the Artesia Light. The story goes that one night, a football player was so frightened by the appearance of the light that he shot at it with his pistol to make it go away. It did. Hundreds of less volatile students have refrained from talking or making any other kind of noise at midnight as they patiently await the ghostly watchman's arrival.

Hundreds of people claim to have seen the Artesia Light over the years. Indeed, this particular ghost light has become one of northeast Mississippi's greatest mysteries. The fact that the tale has been passed down for generations suggests that the mystery will never be solved.

COLUMBUS

HICKORY STICKS

Hickory Sticks is one of oldest—and most private—antebellum homes in Columbus. It was originally built as a dogtrot-style log cabin in 1820 on the top of a heavily wooded hill, making it barely visible from the street. The first owner of the house was Andrew Weir. In the 1840s, Robert Hayden, the first mayor of Columbus, bought the house. He dug the basement and planted vineyards on the estate. Other changes were made during this decade as well, including the addition of a Greek Revival façade, a veranda and tall, square columns. One of the later owners of the house was General Stephen D. Lee. Blewett Lee, Stephen Lee's heir, donated part of the property to the City of Columbus for use as Lee Park. In the twentieth century, plaster was removed from the walls of one of the original rooms, revealing the hewn timbers of the log cabin underneath. According to local legend, one of the early owners of Hickory Sticks is still keeping watch on his former home.

In the 1960s and '70s, the house was occupied by the family of Robert Ivy Sr. His wife, Mrs. Francis Ivy, wrote a column for the *Commercial Dispatch*. In 1968, she told Pat Brooks, a newspaper reporter, about her resident ghost. She said that during the week of Valentine's Day, the ghost always walks through the old part of the house, climbs the stairs and then reenters the same log cabin bedroom each night. Mrs. Ivy distinctly recalled the first time she heard the "Valentine Ghost":

Hickory Sticks is haunted by the Valentine Ghost, which climbs the stairs to the "log cabin bedroom" during Valentine's week.

> *Robert was out of town, and believe me, my sister and I were quite upset. Then when my husband returned the following week, I hesitated to tell him of the incident for fear he would just shrug it off as being a case of two imaginative women alone in a big house. The following year, during the week of Valentine's Day, again, my husband was home, and we both heard him! That made a believer out of Robert for sure!*

For several nights, the Ivys were undisturbed during the night:

> *Things were quiet until along toward the middle of Valentine's week. Then, late one night, my husband and I both sat bolt upright in the bed at almost the exact instance! Our Valentine Ghost was slowly, very slowly, mounting the stairway, and then he entered the log cabin bedroom directly over our room and the door closed.*

For a minute or two, Mr. and Mrs. Ivy sat very still, wondering if their ears had deceived them. "Then my husband jumped out of bed," Mrs. Ivy recalled, "and rushed up the stairs and into the bedroom—but nothing was found. A thorough search of the house also revealed nothing."

Over the years, Mrs. Ivy became accustomed to sharing her home with a ghost, and she began to think of him as part of the family. Her initial fear of the spirit eventually morphed into curiosity. In fact, she was even willing to join the ghost on one of his annual treks through the house if she could find out his name. Mrs. Ivy became so fond of the Valentine Ghost that her greatest fear was that one day he would cease his Valentine's Day visits.

COMMERCIAL DISPATCH

A number of different newspapers served Columbus before the *Commercial Dispatch* came on the scene. The city's first two newspapers came to the city in 1833. The *Southern Argus* represented Henry Clay's National Republican Party, and the *Democratic Press* represented Andrew Jackson's Democratic Party. Three years later, the *Democratic Press* became the *Columbus Democrat*. After the Whig Party took over the *Southern Argus* in 1840, it became the *Columbus Whig*. In 1850, the *Columbus Whig* changed its name to the *Primitive Republican*, which merged with the *Columbus Democrat* a few years later. The *Columbus Democrat* ceased publication during the Civil War but began printing again in 1868. It was bought by the *Columbus Daily Dispatch* in 1879. The editors at this time were W.H. and W.C Worthington. Another newspaper, the *Columbus Index*, which started up in 1865, went through several owners before J.T. Senter acquired the newspaper in 1894 and changed its name to the *Columbus Commercial*. The newspaper was printed in the basement of the old Opera House. The future of the newspaper was threatened by a devastating fire in 1900. Senter not only managed to continue publication of the *Columbus Democrat*, but he even began publishing another newspaper, the *Vicksburg American*. Senter's wife took over the newspaper following her husband's death at age forty-eight. After she died seven years later, her son George changed the name of the newspaper to the *Commercial*.

J.T. Senter's primary competitor was Samuel Thomas Maer, who had prospected for gold in California in 1849 and Australia before settling in Columbus. He bought the *Columbus Dispatch* from Newton Berryhill in 1881. The main office of Maer's newspaper was a small wooden building on Fifth Street. His wife, Susan Maer, began running the newspaper after her husband died. She lived in an apartment inside the newspaper office. Her son, Percy

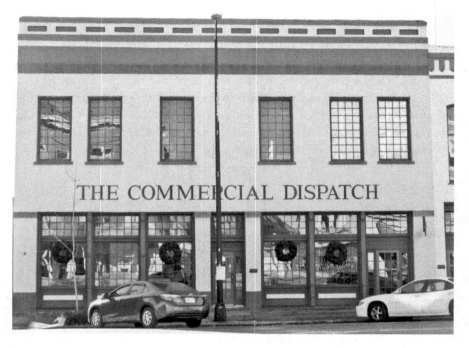

Pressmen working in the basement of the *Commercial Dispatch* hear strange clanging noises and disembodied footsteps.

W. Maer, became owner and publisher of the *Columbus Dispatch* after she retired. Following Percy W. Maer's death, his wife sold the *Commercial Dispatch* to Birney Imes Sr. After Imes purchased the *Columbus Commercial*, he merged the two newspapers in 1922 under the name the *Commercial Dispatch*, the city's first daily newspaper.

The building that now houses the *Commercial Dispatch* has been used for a variety of purposes over the years. At one time, it was used as a farm and equipment shop and at another, as a car dealership. The *Commercial Dispatch* originally occupied the basement and the first floor. Several offices and radio station WCBI were on the second floor. The pressmen working in the basement were the first to report the paranormal activity in the building. They heard strange noises, like clanging sounds and bumps, when no one else was around. Objects that were placed in one spot were moved out of reach when the men were distracted.

A press operator named Jerry Hayes also felt uncomfortable down in the basement. He said that on some nights while working upstairs, he heard the press running when it was supposed to be shut down. He also observed other machines turning themselves on and off. One of Hayes's fellow workers told him that one evening he saw the lower legs of someone walking on the catwalk. The rest of the man's body was obscured by the machinery. The worker walked over to the catwalk, but no one was there.

Another employee, Raymond Blain, reported being unnerved by the sound of the disembodied footsteps of someone wearing hard-soled shoes. He also said that, several times, he caught a glimpse of a white shape in his peripheral vision. However, when he turned his head to look at the figure, it was gone.

Carolyn Burns, one of the founders of Columbus's Ghosts and Legends Tour, had her own paranormal experience inside the *Commercial Dispatch* building. "In 1965, '66, I worked in the advertising department," Carolyn said, "and on Sunday afternoons, on occasion, I would have to come in and do tear sheets. I was always by myself, but I was not by myself 'cause I could hear sounds. I just attributed it to being in an old building and nothing paranormal. But now that I've heard all the stories, maybe that's what it was, and I didn't want to think about it in that way."

One of the strangest incidents occurred in the 1980s. A teenage boy who worked in circulation after school and on weekends was in the building one Saturday night to make sure the newspapers carriers had picked up their papers before six o'clock on Sunday morning. He was alone in the building when, suddenly, he heard voices and what he described as "clacking sounds" coming from the basement. He walked down the stairs to investigate. Convinced that nothing was out of the ordinary in the basement, he walked backed toward the stairs when, in his peripheral vision, he caught a brief glimpse of pool tables, players, lights and spectators. He also heard the clicking of billiard balls. The boy turned his head to get a better look, and the vision disappeared. He knew his mother might be able to help him make sense of what he had just witnessed because of her interest in local history. After he returned home and described the spectral scene to his mother, she recalled seeing an old photograph of a pool hall in a small building west of the *Commercial Dispatch*. A few days later, while she was conducting research in the archives of the public library, the boy's mother, Carolyn Neault, found an old photograph of the building with a sign that read, "Billiards." In that instant, she realized her son had not been imagining things.

Not everyone takes the rumors of the hauntings at the *Commercial Dispatch* seriously. Jerry Hayes's brother, Stan, who also works the presses, was skeptical about the alleged ghosts in the old building. "I've never seen nothing," he told a reporter. Even though Stan thought the ghost stories were nonsense, he was still able to see the potential for humor in his brother's encounters. For a while, he entertained the notion of hiding under a draped plastic sheet or a table and jumping out at people when they entered the room to prove his point: ghosts aren't real.

FRIENDSHIP CEMETERY

The first cemetery in Columbus was established in 1820 south of the original city limits on a bluff above the Tombigbee River. Friendship Cemetery was established in 1849 on five acres of land owned by the Union Lodge No. 35 of the Independent Order of Odd Fellows. The design of the cemetery was inspired by the emblem of the Odd Fellows. The oval driveways formed three interlocking links. In 1869, the Ladies Monumental Association planted magnolia trees along the lane connecting the southwest and northwest burial plots of Confederate soldiers. The United Daughters of the Confederacy planted additional magnolias in 1876.

The first person buried in Friendship Cemetery was Elizabeth Bell Sinclair, the eighteen-year-old wife of Alexander Sinclair. She died in childbirth on July 16, 1849. The graves marked with earlier dates were moved to Friendship Cemetery from older cemeteries, including the grave of William Cocke (1747–1828), an early settler who was a friend of Thomas Jefferson and a veteran of the American Revolution and the Creek Indian War. Other prominent people from Columbus's past are Alexander Bedford Meeks, poet laureate of Alabama; Mississippi governors James Whitfield (1791–1873) and Henry Louis Whitfield (1868–1927); Congressmen Jesse Speigh (1795–1847), James Thomas Harrison (CSA, 1811–1879) and Jehu Amariah Orr (CSA, 1828–1921); Disney Studios animator Josh Meador (1911–1965), who won an Oscar for special effects in *20,000 Leagues Under the Sea*; and Clyde Kilby (1902–1986), an English professor known for his scholarship on C.S. Lewis and J.R.R. Tolkien. The oldest section is located to the left of the second entrance.

Hundreds of veterans of the American Revolution, the War of 1812, the Mexican War, the Civil War, the Spanish-American War, the Korean War and the Vietnam War are buried here as well. Five Confederate generals are laid to rest in Friendship Cemetery, including Lieutenant General Stephen Dill Lee (1833–1908); Brigadier General William Edwin Baldwin (1827–1864); Brigadier General Jeptha Vining Harris (1816–1899); Brigadier

General Jacob Hunter Sharp (1833–1907); and Brigadier General William B. Wade (1823–1866).

Following the Battle of Shiloh (April 6–7, 1862), thousands of wounded Confederate and Union soldiers were transported south via the railroad to field hospitals in towns such as Columbus. Many of the soldiers who did not succumb to their wounds in the railroad cars eventually died of gangrene in the field hospitals. Approximately 2,194 Confederate soldiers were interred in the southwest and the central portions of Friendship Cemetery. The remains of thirty-two Union soldiers are interred here as well. By 1934, 1,260 marble tombstones had been installed, but only 47 of those were inscribed with names. Thanks to the discovery of older record books in 1976, the names of an additional 298 soldiers and 1 nurse were inscribed on marble markers.

On April 25, 1866, four women from Columbus—Mrs. Augusta Murdock Sykes Cox, Mrs. Frances Jane Butler Garrrett Fontaine, Mrs. Kate McCarthy Hill Cooper Heath and Mrs. Martha Elizabeth Morton—placed flowers on the graves of the Union and Confederate dead. Their selfless gesture was commemorated in "The Blue and the Grey," a poem written by New England poet Francis White Finch and published in September 1867 in the *Atlantic Monthly*. Their remembrance of their fallen husbands, fathers and brothers is now recognized as the first observance of what has come to be known as Memorial Day.

Today, Friendship Cemetery encompasses approximately fifteen thousand graves on sixty acres. Since 1991, students at the Mississippi School of Mathematics and Science have dramatized the lives of a number of people buried in Friendship Cemetery in a tour called "Tales from the Crypt." Visitors to the old cemetery

This monument in Friendship Cemetery commemorates the beginning of Memorial Day on April 25, 1866, when four women placed flowers on the graves of Union and Confederate soldiers.

A spectral soldier is said to patrol the graves of Confederate soldiers in Friendship Cemetery.

stop at specific grave sites and listen to the students, dressed in period clothing, re-create the lives of the people buried there. However, Friendship Cemetery does not appeal just to history lovers. People fascinated by ghost legends and folklore visit the old graveyard as well.

One of the old cemetery's most frequently told ghost stories has to do with the section of the cemetery where Confederate soldiers are buried. Many people claim to have spotted the specter of a Confederate soldier patrolling the graves of his fallen comrades. Ghost-hunting groups who have investigated the story have found it difficult to prove or disprove. The large number of sightings does seem to give the tale some credence, though.

A much more whimsical ghost story focuses on Mrs. Munroe's white brick mausoleum. Supposedly, when someone approaches the old tomb and calls out, "Mrs. Munroe, Mrs. Munroe, what are you doing?" she replies, "Nothing at all." Variations of this story can be found all over the South.

Without a doubt, the most legendary—and photographed—tombstone in Friendship Cemetery is the "Angel of Grief." This term is used to describe monuments erected in the style of sculptor William Wetmore Story's creation.

Legend has it that the ghost of Mrs. Munroe responds if one knocks on her mausoleum and asks, "Mrs. Munroe, what are you doing?"

The Angel of Grief is the most photographed monument in Friendship Cemetery.

These dramatic statues can be found all over the world. The Angel of Grief in Friendship Cemetery marks the grave of Reverend Thomas Cox Teasdale, the ninth pastor of First Baptist Church in Columbus, who died in 1891 at the age of eighty-three. This particular monument was created by the firm of J.L. Miller in Quincy, Maine. Many visitors to Friendship Cemetery have remarked about the lifelike texture of the statue's arms. A few have felt as if the angel's eyes followed them as they walked past the grave.

Proof of the hauntings may have surfaced in 2008. Matt Garner, a page designer for the *Commercial Dispatch*, was in the habit of taking photographs inside Friendship Cemetery in his off hours. One morning, around sunrise, Garner set up his camera on his tripod, just as he had done many times, and pointed the camera east. He then took ten photographs, hoping to catch the sunlight filtering through the limbs of a magnolia tree and forming shadows on the tombstones of Confederate soldiers. When Garner examined the photographs, he was shocked to see the transparent image of a dark face with hollow eyes in the center of one of the photographs. A hint of a grin can be detected. The transparent face showed up in only one of the ten photographs Garner shot that morning.

ARBOR HOUSE

Formerly known as the Cady House, Arbor House is a pastel green Italianate town house located at 518 College Street. In its first stage, Arbor House was a two-room cottage built by Benjamin Toomer in 1840. Colonel William Cady bought the home in 1841. Cady owned two livery stables, one across the street from his home and the other, called the Eclipse, in what is now known as Cady Hills. Cady also ran a hotel and owned one of the city's first plumbing businesses. Arbor House became the impressive mansion that stands today sometime after 1854. The old house was renamed by Michael and Sheila Jessyl, importers of Victorian antiques.

In the early 2000s, the *Rick and Bubba* radio show sent a team of ghost hunters to Arbor House to investigate the reported hauntings in the old house. Team members focused their investigation on the Gentlemen's Parlor, where the master of the house and his friends entertained themselves after dinner parties with cigars, strong drinks and such

In Arbor House, pictures of women never stay hung in the Gentlemen's Parlor.

"manly" topics of discussion as politics. The ladies' parlor in antebellum mansions was reserved for the mistress of the house and her friends, who drank tea, shared the latest gossip and sewed. Over the years, various owners of Arbor House swore that if they hung any portraits or photographs of women in the Gentlemen's Parlor, they would find them the next morning lying on a table or chair with the wire and nail intact.

The ghost-hunting group hung a print of a woman on the wall of the Gentleman's Parlor and set up its EMF detectors, motion detectors and video cameras. The group then left the room and set up equipment in other parts of the house. The members of the group were investigating the west parlor when, suddenly, the motion detectors went off. They ran into the room and were disappointed to find the print of the lady still hanging on the wall. However, a cat standing in the doorway arched its back, snarled and ran out of the room. The investigators left Arbor House convinced that they had stirred up something in the Gentlemen's Parlor.

THE PRINCESS THEATER

The Kuykendall family name has become synonymous with the theater in Columbus. Ed Kuykendall Sr. (1888–1946) opened an open-air theater in Columbus—the Princess Airdome—in 1917. Three years later, Kuykendall opened an in-door theater on Fifth Street. In 1923, work began on a much grander theater: the Princess. When construction was completed in 1924, the *Commercial Dispatch* called the 1,200-seat theater "the handsomest and costliest theater in Mississippi." The theater's stage, one of the largest in the state, was sixty-four by thirty-four feet. It opened as a vaudeville house and later became a movie theater. The silent film *The Black Oxen*, starring Corrine Griffith, Conway Tearles and Clara Bow, was shown at the theater's grand opening. Broadway shows such as *Blossom Time*, *Rio Rita*, *Broadway Melody*, *Merry Widow* and *42nd Street* were also performed here. Musical accompaniment for the shows was provided in an orchestra pit in front of the stage. The organ pipes ran along the walls. Two organists played during the showing of silent movies and at intermission. Will Rogers and other stars of the 1920s and '30s appeared on the stage. Admission for road shows was $3.50. Customers paid $0.25 to attend regular showings and Saturday matinees. Kuykendall's wife, Ophelia, said that there were never any long-run movies at the Princess Theater: "We changed programs every day. Friday night was our biggest night, for that's when we showed western shows featuring Gene Autry, and stars like that." Although road shows traveled with most of their own stage equipment and props, the Princess Theater had its own murals and backdrops. The small building adjacent to the Princess Theater was a tearoom, where theatergoers could sit at small round tables and partake of delicious concoctions from the soda fountain after the performances.

Kuykendall was elected president of the Motion Pictures Theater Owners of America in 1932, a position he held until his death in 1946. Because of Kuykendall's connections in the film industry, a number of other Hollywood celebrities visited Columbus, such as Clark Gable, who stayed at the Columbus Air Force Base for a weekend. The Princess Theater has the distinction of being the first theater in Mississippi to show *Gone with the Wind* in 1939. In 1938, Kuykendall leased the Princess Theater to MALCO Theaters, which operated the facility until around 1970. After MALCO relinquished its lease, Mrs. Kuykendall ran the Princess as a community theater. The City of Columbus considered buying the Princess Theater on several occasions in the 1980s and '90s,

Paranormal investigators photographed the image of a shadowy figure in the balcony of the Princess Theater.

but plans fell through. The theater stood empty for a while, until it was purchased by Dr. Mark Burtman in 2006. Today, the old theater is used for live performances and concerts. It's also a popular investigation site for ghost-hunting groups.

The apparition that has been sighted at the Princess Theater is said to be the ghost of Ed Kuykendall Sr. In the late 2000s, a group of paranormal investigators captured the image of a shadowy figure in the balcony. The theater has such a haunted reputation that a Ghost Hunters Convention was held there on September 7–9, 2007. Jeff Harris, a parapsychologist who organized the weekend of classes, lectures and tours, said that he had recorded a number of intriguing EVPs at the Princess Theater. The ghostly activity at the Princess Theater may be the result of the renovations, which occurred in 1941, 1984, 1993 and 2006. Whatever was "awakened" during the periods of rejuvenation shows no indication of wanting to take a "final bow" at the Princess Theater.

ROSEDALE

With the exception of the transom over the front door, which is Federal style in design, Rosedale's architectural style is "pure" Italianate. Dr. William Topp seem to have been influenced by *The Model Architect*, a book published by Philadelphia architect Samuel Sloan. Dr. Topp may have met Sloan in 1853, when the architect was beginning work on Bryce Hospital in Tuscaloosa, Alabama. Built of brick and stucco, the mansion was completed around 1855. Its most distinctive exterior features are its bell tower, piazza and flat roof. The Italianate features include the canopied balcony, the decorative wooden tracery and the Venetian arch windows on each side of the third-floor tower. Dr. Topp believed that building his mansion in a pastoral setting enhanced its beauty. Architectural historians have proclaimed Rosedale to be one of the finest examples of Italianate architecture in the entire state.

A great deal of thought went into furnishing the interior of Rosedale, as well. Craftsmen from New Orleans were hired to create the home's unique furnishings. Rococo Revival– and Empire-style furniture, with their shades

Rosedale was built in the Italianate style for Dr. William Topp in 1855.

Many of the rooms in Rosedale, like the parlor, contain Rococo Revival and Empire furniture.

of greens, blues and gold tones, calls to mind the Mediterranean designs that were part of Dr. Topp's inspiration for his Italianate mansion.

After leaving Nashville, Dr. Topp lived temporarily in Pulaski, Tennessee, before finally settling in Columbus. He did not practice medicine while living in Columbus. Instead, he held a variety of positions, such as manager of his brother-in-law's land and member of a bank board and local college board. Later on, he became a land speculator and a planter.

Following his death, Dr. Topp's three eldest children—Ann Lacy, Bettie and Hugh—sold the house to their two younger siblings, Ozella and William W. Jr., the latter of whom built his own home in 1902. William's children sold Rosedale to W.V. Grace and his wife, Beatrice, on May 20, 1904. Mary Grace Wood Anderson bought the home after William V. Grace died. She and her husband lived in Rosedale with their two daughters until 1946. Mary Grace Wood Anderson sold the house to Richard Powell Fleming on April 15, 1946. He purchased the old house as a present to his son. Fleming was also interested in using the gravel on the property for his gravel business. He lived in Rosedale with his wife, Mary McGuire Fleming; a daughter, Katherine; another daughter, Mary Linda; and a son, Richard Powell Jr. Mrs. Fleming sold

A guest spending the night in this second-floor bedroom was frightened by the image of a little girl standing in the hallway.

Rosedale to Terry Stubblefield and his wife, Deborah, in August 1993. The couple made a number of improvements to the old house, including removing the old electricity and plumbing and closing off some of the closets. In 1998, the Stubblefields sold the house to Gene and Leigh Imes, who have furnished Rosedale with antiques dating back to its period of construction.

Rosedale has been known as a haunted house since the 1940s. Between 1940 and 1946, neighborhood children told Mary Grace Wood Anderson that they saw lights in the tower. They also claimed to have seen a shadowy figure climbing the stairs as they peered through one of the first-story windows. Mrs. Anderson never indicated that she believed these fantastic tales, but she refused to climb the stairs to the tower.

Years later, a visitor spent the night in one of the upstairs bedrooms. He had not been asleep for very long when he was awakened by the image of a woman and a little girl standing in the hallway. They were wearing clothing dating back to the late nineteenth century. The next morning, when he was asked if he had spent a pleasant night in the room, he replied, "I will never come back to this house again!" Apparently, he was true to his word.

ALDAN HALL

Aldan Hall, a Greek Revival home at 901 Seventh Avenue North, was built as a town house in 1839 for John Topp, one of the first trustees at the Columbus Female Institute. The house was purchased by James Sykes in 1854. Over the years, a number of additions were made to the four-room house, including the addition of a west wing and a Federal-style portico with two octagonal columns. The new owners also moved the staircase to the newly constructed side hall. As a result of the alterations, the modest town house had now acquired an L shape.

Wayne and Betty Bryan bought the house in 1982 and named it Aldan Hall for their two sons. By the time they finally took possession of the abandoned house, it had undergone a number of other changes. The couple immediately set about repairing the damage incurred by years of neglect. While working on the house, the Bryans made several interesting discoveries. They were examining the front doors when they realized that the original owners were able to "air condition" the house by removing the side lights

The owners of Aldan Hall sensed that someone was watching them from the balcony not long after they moved in.

and transom. The couple found a planter in the form of a magnetic compass under the patio. They also found the signature of architect/builder James Lull on a walnut newel post on a staircase and a trapdoor leading from the front hall to the basement. However, their most startling discovery was the presence of ghosts in their fine old home.

Wayne and Betty sensed that they were not alone in the house soon after they moved in. They felt like someone—or something—was watching them from the balcony. They also began hearing the creaking of footsteps in the upstairs foyer and phantom footsteps in the hallway. Mrs. Bryan believed that the gentle ghost inhabiting her home was the mournful spirit of Marcella Jane Sykes Lanier, whose life was rife with tragedy. Not only was her husband killed in the Civil War in 1861, but her first two children died in infancy as well. She herself died young a few years later without seeing her two remaining children reach adulthood. Martha Neyman, a staff writer for the *Commercial Dispatch*, speculated that Mrs. Lanier's ghost "is peering over the balcony railing thinking she hears her husband's voice or calling her children to come upstairs."

WHITEHALL

Whitehall at 607 Third Street once occupied the entire city block. The Colonial home was built in 1843 for Judge Harris, a planter who was originally from Georgia. The two-story home has a corbeled chimney top, plaster placed between the windows, a balcony, six-over-six double-hung windows, dentils, six square box columns on the portico and a hip roof capped with a belvedere. The interior of the home is graced with a Greek Revival doorway, colored glass sidelights and a pine floor. The house is furnished with a number of rare antiques. Several outbuildings still stand in the rear yard, including stables, a carriage house and servants' quarters. Colorful gardens decorate the manicured lawns. This was clearly a home for one of the city's most prominent citizens.

However, Whitehall has not always been a showplace. It served as a field hospital for Confederate soldiers during the Civil War. During World Ward II, the Greek Revival mansion was converted into a servicemen's club called the Drop-In Hangar. A collection of wartime Disney cartoon images hung from the walls, including one inscribed, "Happy Landings at Whitehall, Walt Disney."

Built for Judge Harries in 1843, Whitehall served as a field hospital in the Civil War and as a servicemen's club in World War II.

Whitehall had one of the first modern bathrooms in Columbus. Family members brushed their teeth in the mouth-washing sink. The children, who spent most of the day running around barefoot, washed their feet in the foot-washing tub, which had running water. Everything in the bathroom is original, with the exception of the toilet.

In 2006, the present owner of White Hall, Mrs. Carol Boggess, was sitting in the kitchen, waiting for a reporter to take photographs of her home. As she was gazing out one of the windows, she saw what appeared to be the white figure of a woman passing by. Instead of gasping with astonishment or screaming, she was privileged to have had an experience that few people have had. "I was thrilled to have seen a ghost," she said.

The interior of Whitehall seems to be haunted, as well. In the first bedroom to the right of the door, the light has turned itself off and on several times. Adding to the mystery is the fact that the light switch is difficult to turn on. Apparently, the mischievous entity is going through a great deal of trouble to make its presence known.

The most haunted room in Whitehall is the master bedroom, which was originally the ballroom. One night during the period when the old house was

Above: Whitehall had the first modern bathroom in Columbus. The owners brushed their teeth in the mouth-washing sink, and children washed their feet in the foot-washing tub.

Left: The light in this bedroom has turned on by itself several times.

being remodeled, the owner's son fell asleep in one of the other bedrooms. Suddenly, he was awakened by the sound of waltz music coming from the old ballroom across the hall, which was being remodeled at the time. When he told his mother what had happened, she asked if the music could have come from someone carrying a boombox across the street. He replied, "No, Mom. I play the violin, and I know waltz music when I hear it."

Ghosts have manifested themselves in Whitehall in other ways, as well. One day, Mrs. Boggess invited another reporter to walk around the house, taking photographs. Later, when the reporter examined the photographs closely, he was startled to find orbs flitting about in several of the pictures. As far as Mrs. Boggess is concerned, the ghost stories only add to the allure of her beautiful home.

OLE MAGNOLIA

The Greek Revival home at 1219 Third Avenue North was built in 1854. Bernard Hendricks deeded the property to Lucy Ann Sharp on November 23, 1858, for $4,000. Lucy and her husband, Elisha, owned the house from 1858 to January 9, 1863. Their three children were Thomas J., Caroline S. and Jacob H. Sharp. During the Civil War, Jacob was appointed captain of the Tombigbee Rangers. While her husband was fighting for the Confederacy, Lucy sold all of Block 83 to Harriet Ward for $4,500. John Brownrigg bought the west half of Block 83 on March 12, 1887. On March 12, 1892, Morris and Maggie paid Harriet $2,000 for the east half of Block 83. In 1900, David Stewart McClanahan and his wife, Jontee, purchased the home. The couple spent the next five years adding a second story to the house to accommodate their five boys and five girls. The McClanahans became one of the city's most prominent families. David Stewart McClanahan served as mayor of Columbus from 1917 to 1921; his son H.H. McClanahan served as mayor from 1945 to 1947.

During the 1930s, one of the McClanahans' daughters, Ruthie, converted the house to apartments. The large front columns were added, and the wraparound porch was removed. The McClanahan family owned the apartment house until November 11, 1977, when James Lancaster bought the home. He, in turn, sold the house to Thomas Michael Smith on August 21, 1979. He made a number of improvements on the house, including the conversion of the back porch into a family room. The next owners, Robert

The mischievous ghost that haunts Ole Magnolia enjoys opening locked doors.

and Wand Gatlin, added vinyl siding in 1983. In November 1990, Charles and Jan Bullock bought the old home. On October 10, 1992, a storm did considerable damage to the house. The wind tore holes in the roof and shattered fifty-two windowpanes. Afterward, the Bullocks found shards of glass embedded in the walls and piles of pecan leaves in the corners of the rooms. Over the next two years, the couple set about renovating the historic home. They refinished the wooden floors, replaced the carpets, reworked the windows and installed imported English wallcoverings in the dining room. The Bullocks also laid new hardwood floors in the family room and installed a new window, wainscoting and two new double-entry French doors. Exterior work included reworking the front balcony and the addition of a new green roof and two new porches. A three-car garage was built as well. The Bullocks' efforts were recognized in 1994, when Ole Magnolia won the Most Improved Residence title.

Like many owners of antebellum homes, the Bullocks gave names to the refinished rooms: Rosewood Parlor, the Magnolia Room, the Gettysburg Dining Room, the Butler's Pantry and the Riverbend. Their attempt to restore Ole Magnolia to its former glory may have disturbed the spirit of one of the previous owners. Jan Bullock witnessed a male spirit on two occasions: "The first time was when we started the renovation of the upstairs west side. A male figure walked out of the green bedroom into some mattresses standing in the hall and vanished. He was seen several months later sitting at the top of the stairs. He got up and walked in the office and vanished again." Jan theorized that belief in the paranormal played a large role in its manifestations:

> We feel he had to trust us before revealing himself to us. . . . He has not revealed himself to me. I am a little tense of the situation, and I think he knows that. He will not show himself to our daughters when they visited from college because they, too, are afraid. This is why I say he is a good ghost. He only revealed himself to my husband and another lady because they believed in him.

Even though Jan lost her fear of the ghost over the next few months, he never appeared to her, possibly because she was afraid of him at one time. The Bullocks' dog, on the other hand, never really got used to sharing the house with a ghost: "There are times when our little dog will not go upstairs, and she lies down and looks at the stairs as if someone is standing there."

Despite the ghost's unnerving interruptions of normalcy in the Bullock household, the couple never really felt threatened by the spirit's mischievous acts, such as playing with the front door:

> When my husband and I moved into the home, we locked the front door, and on several occasions we would come down the stairs to find the front door standing wide open. After a few words on who left the door unlocked, we would make sure the door was locked. [Then we would] come down the next day to find it standing wide open. The only time he cannot open the door is when it is chain locked. He has not opened the door since he made his appearance.

Jan Bullock believed that the ghost keeps the house from harm and that she and her husband released him to watch over it once again. In 2011, Ole Magnolia passed into the hands of Lee and Pete Tortorici, who, like Charles and Jan Bullock, immediately fell in love with the grand old home. They adorned Ole Magnolia with artwork and antiques, including an eighteenth-century sideboard. "Every addition was done with such intelligence," Lee said. "The house has an incredibly warm feel to it. It's very obvious that it's been deeply loved and appreciated." One could argue that love for the old home is also behind the haunting of Ole Magnolia.

DOWSING-BANKS-FOOTE-MAHON-HUDSON HOME

The old house at 820 Seventh Avenue North was built in 1840 by Major William Dowsing, who came to Columbus from Georgia in 1822. Dowsing was a veteran of the War of 1812 and a devout Methodist who led the singing in his church. He was also a businessman who operated a tavern and store on Main Street. He was the county's first clerk of the circuit court, land registrar and a trustee of the Franklin Academy. Dowsing needed a large house to accommodate his four sons and seven daughters. In later years, the size of the house attracted a number of other couples with large families. In 1850, Major Dowsing sold the property to Dunstan Banks, who had moved

Captain H.D. Foote's ghost appears to be unhappy about the conversion of the Dowsing-Banks-Foote-Mahon-Hudson Home into an apartment building.

to Columbus from a farm west of the Tombigbee River. Banks had four children: Robert W., Lutie, Julia and Henrietta. The next owner, Robert W. Banks, also had four children: Sarah Felix, Lucille, Robert W. Jr. and James Oliver Banks. The next owner of the house was Captain H.D. Foote, who had six children: William, George, Annette, Sally, Henry and Sue. Several different people owned the house after Captain Foote's death, including Mrs. Mahon and Mr. James Hudson. Eventually, the old house became an apartment house. Today, the front of the house is blocked by other houses built on the square.

The entity haunting the Dowsing-Banks-Foote-Mahon-Hudson Home is said to be the spirit of Captain H.D. Foote, who, apparently, was not a colorful character. No one knows for sure why the ghostly presence has been determined to be the spirit of Captain Foote. For many years, occupants of the old house have heard the heavy footsteps of a male figure pacing back and forth, almost as if he were deep in thought. During a twenty-year period, James Caswell Hudson reared his family of four boys and a girl in the old house. According to Mrs. Russell Hudson, the boys always stopped at the foot of the stairs and listened for any strange sounds before walking upstairs. Mrs. Hudson said that even though she came to the old home as a bride, she never heard the ghost of Captain Foote. She suspected that the fate of the antebellum home might be the cause of Captain Foote's unhappiness: "Could it be that Captain Foote foresaw the sad conclusion of his once proud home? His unhappy striding back and forth surely showed he was disturbed and wanted the present occupants to share his unhappiness."

WHITE ARCHES

A wealthy planter named Jeptha Vining Harris built White Arches at 122 Seventh Avenue South in 1857. He left his native Georgia and arrived in Mississippi in 1840, shortly after his marriage to Mary Oliver Banks. Harris, whose family had been actively involved in Georgia politics, was elected to the Mississippi state legislature in 1856. During the Civil War, Harris raised his own regiment and was appointed to the rank of brigadier general.

White Arches is unlike any antebellum home in Columbus, owing to its eclectic architectural features. Greek Revival influences are evident in the wide central hall flanked by large square rooms on both sides. The typical key Greek design can be seen in the millwork and in the dentil cornices

Paint does not adhere to the walls of one of the rooms in White Arches.

as well. The sloping metal roof is supported by Gothic arches. The center columns were fashioned in the Italianate style.

This three-level mansion has a number of other unique elements as well. The books lining a floor-to-ceiling walnut bookcase in the library reflect Harris's scholarly interests. The library also has ceiling rosette, a marble mantel and frosted glass sidelights. A cross hall separates the library from the central hall. A large mahogany staircase was installed in the front hall; a small spiral staircase in a small hall in the rear of the house leads to the four bedrooms on the second floor. The bedroom closets were a unique feature for that time. An observatory and central octagonal tower are supported by the central columns. The majority of the doors are double doors with glass panes and stained- and satin glass sidelights. Four of these double doors lead from the tower to a wrought-iron balcony. The corner posts of the gallery railing are topped by decorative brass balls. None of the doors on the exterior side of the balconies and porches have knobs. A number of outbuildings still exist behind the main house: the laundry room, the kitchen, slaves' quarters, an ice cellar and a storage room.

Owing to its spaciousness, White Arches became one of the social centers of Columbus. In fact, one of the city's last "old-time parties" was held there.

The night before the Columbus Riflemen left for war, most of the social elite of Columbus attended sixteen-year-old Mary Oliver Harris's debut party at White Arches. Soldiers in full dress uniforms and ladies wearing jeweled necklaces and satin dresses glided through the spacious parlor and dining room; couples walking hand in hand strolled through the double doors leading to the galleries. Most of the guests were in high spirits, insulated—for a brief time—from the misery and suffering soon to come. No one wanted to think about the probability that some of these young men would not be returning to their loved ones.

Legend has it that the lavish party did not bode well for Mary Oliver Harris. The story goes that Mary Oliver's parents threw the party to raise her spirits. She was despondent over her beau's impending departure for the battlefield. During the party, Mary Oliver climbed the stairs to the balcony to get a breath of fresh air. Breathing the cold night air chilled the poor girl, and she caught a severe cold. The cold eventually developed into pneumonia, and Mary Oliver died. Supposedly, her parents were so grief-stricken that they could not abide the thought of living in the house where their daughter died. Not long thereafter, they sold the house and moved away.

Stories that White Arches might be haunted were confirmed in the late twentieth century, when Mrs. Joanne Leicke moved into the old mansion. Just before purchasing the house, she asked the realtor if the house was haunted. "She said 'yes.' This made me very happy because I'd always wanted to live in a haunted house," Mrs. Leicke said. Her first paranormal encounter occurred the first night she was alone in the house. She and her dog had just gone to bed when, suddenly, she heard a loud racket upstairs: doors slamming and the grating noise of furniture being moved around. "I got my dog and sat down on the couch in the entry way and waited it out until the noise stopped," Mrs. Leicke said. "Then I went to bed. At the time, my dog didn't seem to be upset. A few minutes later, the noises started up again. The lights wouldn't come on, so I got my flashlight and went upstairs. Nothing had been moved." Mrs. Leicke returned to her bedroom, hoping that the noises would cease and she would get a good night's sleep. She had just drifted off to sleep when the dog started growling, as if someone were standing outside the door. Determined not to let anything chase her out of her house, Mrs. Leicke went to the foot of the stairs and yelled, "This is my house! I'm not afraid, and you had better accept me." Mrs. Leicke's defiance worked. She did not hear any more noises during the night.

Mrs. Leicke said that one dark, wintry evening, she was painting one of the upstairs room when, suddenly, the tightly shut bedroom door slowly opened all by itself. Undeterred, Mrs. Leicke continued painting. However, she was completely baffled when the paint refused to adhere to one of the walls. Over the next few weeks, she and her husband made several other attempts to paint the wall but without success. After researching the history of the house, Mrs. Leicke reached the conclusion that the spirit of Mary Oliver Harris did not want the wallpaper stripped from the walls of her bedroom.

After having a number of unnerving experiences, Mrs. Leicke decided to invite a Catholic priest over to her house. "I asked him to bless the house," Mrs. Leicke said. "The priest said he had done some exorcisms in some of the other houses [in Columbus], but I didn't want one." Apparently, Mrs. Leicke and the ghost of Mary Oliver have arrived at some sort of agreement.

THE LINCOLN HOME

Barney B. Lincoln moved to Noxubee County, Mississippi, in 1835 with his wife of one year, Rebecca. The couple settled in Columbus in 1846 and built themselves a home at 714 South Third Avenue. Barney and Rebecca had six children: James F., Armstead Thomas, Barney B. Jr., Susannah, Cicero L. and Henrietta. Cicero, who was brought to the house when he was two years old, remained there for the next ninety-three years.

Cicero Lincoln volunteered to fight in the Confederate army and served until the end of the war. Beginning in 1865, he entered the world of politics, becoming a circuit clerk, a chancery clerk, a member of the Trustees of City Schools, deputy sheriff and sheriff. Two years earlier, when the United States declared war against Spain, Lincoln enlisted in the U.S. Army. He achieved the rank of captain and stayed with his unit until December 1898. Lincoln was appointed colonel during his service in the Mississippi National Guard. Upon his return home, Lincoln read law at night and passed the bar examination in 1900. Lincoln was elected mayor of Columbus in 1901. He was said to have been an amateur historian whose library included a large collection of rare books. He continued practicing law in Columbus until his death in 1939. Lincoln and his wife, Tessie, had eight children, six of whom—Atwell, Berton, Norman, C.L., Lonnie and Sue Mae—lived to adulthood.

The Lincoln Home is a typical mid-nineteenth-century cottage in the A.J. Downing architectural style with its rectangular shape, hipped roof, single gable and perfectly styled chimneys. The roof is supported by four

A woman spending the night at the Lincoln Home was awakened by the ghost of a woman sitting on the edge of her bed.

Greek-style columns. In 1846, the dining room and kitchen were in the brick basement. In later years, the dining room and kitchen were moved to the main floor. Another change that was made to the original structure was the addition of a kitchen, a glassed-in sleeping porch and a bathroom. Another bathroom was added between two bedrooms on the east side of the house. The front door is framed by panes of blue Venetian-styled glass.

The Lincoln Home remained in the Lincoln family for over 120 years. It is now owned by Sid Carradine, who notes, "The Lincoln Home was the carriage/guest house for the Amzi Love House. My wife, Brenda, and I turned it into a bed-and-breakfast about twenty years ago. The house was sold to the Lincolns, and Mr. Lincoln added on to it." The most commonly sighted ghost in the old house is the specter of a woman in a white dress. Guests claim to have seen her walking through the hallways. A few guests have seen a black and gray cloud floating around the parlor. The ghost also makes its presence known through sound. Frequently, the doorbell "clicks" on its own, indicating that someone is standing outside the door. However, when the door is opened, no one is to be found.

A few guests have had startling encounters with the woman in white. Author Jill Pascoe tells the story of two women who were spending the night in the Lincoln Home. One of the women woke up in the middle of the night. As she wiped the sleep out of her eyes, she saw the image of a woman wearing a white, lacy dress sitting on the edge of the bed. Because the dress had ruffles, the woman observed that her friend had changed her nightgown. Her curiosity changed abruptly to fear when she heard her friend snoring. At that instant, the apparition vanished.

Sid Carradine's wife, Brenda, became convinced that the Lincoln Home was haunted on Christmas Day 2005. The ghost she saw, however, did not resemble a human being: "A foggy gray-black shape floated through the parlor toward the mantel from the front hallway and then reversed and went back through the French doors to the hallway." The three other people who were seated in the dining room were transfixed by the look on the face of their hostess. They asked her what had just happened, but she wouldn't say. "I refused to tell them because who would believe it?" she said.

Six years later, Tiffany Hankins, along with her sister and mother, experienced what can be best described as poltergeist activity in one of the downstairs rooms known as the "Tack Room." It was a rainy day, so they decided to stay inside and watch movies. That night, Tiffany and her mother slept in the double bed, and her sister slept in the single bed. Tiffany, who had trouble sleeping, heard someone in the room above climb out of bed, walk to the bathroom, flush the toilet and return to bed. Tiffany heard these noises twice during the night, but she thought nothing of them because she assumed Brenda was sleeping in the room above. Over breakfast, Tiffany asked Brenda if she'd had a rough night. Brenda replied that she had spent the night with her husband in the Amzi Love House next door. No one was sleeping in the room above the Tack Room on that particular night. "I was quite amazed but not frightened," Tiffany said. "I never once felt scared in the house, but I could feel a presence."

Jill Pascoe had her own uncanny experience in January 2011, when she stayed at the Lincoln Home with her mother: "We were standing by the back door of the home, talking with Brenda about the houses, when suddenly, the light at the bottom of the stairs flickered off and on one time. We were not moving, and Brenda said it had never happened before." Most of the time, random occurrences such as this have a rational explanation, such as faulty wiring. In the case of the Lincoln Home, however, where so many strange things happen, an "irrational" explanation seems appropriate.

LIBERTY HALL

Liberty Hall was built by William Ethelbert Ervin, who was born in Sumter District, South Carolina, on September 28, 1809. His parents, Eliza and William Dick Ervin, moved their family to Lowndes County, Mississippi, in 1831. William Ervin bought four thousand acres of land at $1.25 per acre west of Columbus. Historical records indicate that William E. Ervin lived on the farm with his father on the west side of the Tombigbee River until he bought his own land in 1836. The house was built by either Silas McBee between 1827 and 1836 or Ervin himself not long after he acquired the property in 1836. The first addition to the two-story frame house was made before 1839. Work on the dining room and the pantry was completed between 1846 and 1856. An artist from South Carolina came to Liberty Hall to paint the French country scenes on the upper panels of the dining room. Several of the paintings are unfinished because he was forced to leave by the outbreak of the Civil War.

The journals William E. Ervin kept between 1839 and 1856 provide a window into daily life at Ervin's farm, Liberty Hall Plantation. The journals contain information about providing his slaves with blankets, hats and other articles of clothing and paying slaves for working on Christmas Day. The journals also include the duties of husbands and wives, records of his saw- and gristmill, rules for settling quarrels and a requirement that slaves return to their quarters by 9:00 p.m. Facts about his personal life can also be found in the journal. For example, he mentions that he regularly attended church and Sunday school and that, in 1850, he and his wife, Sarah, treated four of their children for a sickness of some sort. One of the children may have had typhoid fever.

Liberty Hall remained in the Ervin family well into the twentieth century. William E. Ervin's son, Dr. Frank Ervin, inherited the property in 1878. The house then passed into the hands of the Armstrong family beginning with J.T. Armstrong in 1901 and Sarah Armstrong in 1915. One of the later owners of the house, Sarah Fowler, explained how the house was moved to its present location:

> *During the hard times around the 1920s, my grandmother [Sarah Armstrong] was a widow and had begun supplementing her income through the sale of gravel dug on the place. The people who were excavating the gravel got closer to the house and soon discovered a wealth of gravel under the house. They asked Grandmother if they could move her house,*

The great-granddaughters of William E. Ervin, the builder of Liberty Hall, saw two misty figures floating along the picket fence.

and she said no because her great-grandmother had brought the boxwoods and other landscaping shrubs all the way from South Carolina! And there was the schoolhouse, smokehouse and other buildings that would have to be moved, too. It was just impossible. Well, as it happened, a cyclone hit in 1921 and destroyed the landscaping and the outbuildings. Grandmother decided that the cyclone was a "sign" from above, so she let them move the house.

The house was moved, inch by inch, by lifting it onto rollers using one mule and a winch. The absence of electricity and plumbing in the house made the move somewhat easier. Descendants of the Ervin family joked that Liberty Hall was the first "mobile home."

A number of changes were made in Liberty Hall over the years. Originally, the house consisted of two downstairs rooms and two upstairs rooms. The kitchen was detached. As the Ervin family grew, a number of additions were made to the house, including a back hall, back stairs, two bedrooms downstairs and two upstairs, a dining room hall and a porch. In some respects, Liberty Hall is a typical planter's home with its façade dominated by a central pediment and four square columns. However, unlike many antebellum homes, Liberty Hall is not adorned with ornate plaster molding. In fact, the only formal part of the house is the parlor. Several members of the Ervin family were laid to rest in a small family cemetery to the far right of the front of the house. According to family legend, at least one of these people is not resting very peacefully.

The first report of haunted activity in the family cemetery came from Carol Armstrong, the great-granddaughter of William Ethelbert Ervin. She said that when she and her sister were young, they saw two misty, humanlike figures gliding along the picket fence. Terrified, the girls ran inside the house to get their father. However, by the time they returned to the place where they saw the ghost, the figure was gone. Ms. Armstrong theorized that because the family cemetery was at one end of the fence, the specters had been surveying the old plantation on a late afternoon walk.

Their curiosity aroused, the girls decided to investigate the possibility that the interior of the house might be haunted as well. A few weeks later, the girls sneaked out of bed and began walking down the dark corridors. They were moving through the "winter corridor" of the old house when, in the flickering light of their candles, they saw what appeared to be a female figure strolling down the hallway. The girls screamed and ran back to their bedrooms. The next morning, they were looking at paintings of their ancestors when they recognized the face of the apparition they had seen the night before: Molly Ervin, William Ethelbert Ervin's daughter.

In the late twentieth century, Fran Fowler Hazard also had an eerie encounter in Liberty Hall. One night, she had just fallen asleep when she had a rude awakening: "I sensed that there was someone there while I was sleeping. And when I woke up, I could see someone sitting on the corner of the bed. He was an old man with white hair. I could not see who it was, but I felt the bed move when he sat down." It seems that the original occupants of Liberty Hall are having difficulty relinquishing their beloved home to the new owners.

HIGHLAND HOUSE

Highland House at 810 Highland Circle occupies the former site of Lindamood, a beautiful antebellum home built by C.F. Sherrod in 1862. The furnishings were said to be magnificent. Eighteen months were required

A group of paranormal investigators photographed the ghostly image of a face in the mirror at Highland House.

to complete the fresco work alone. All of the molding was handmade by a skilled artisan named Kliona, who was brought from the North to complete the work. The house had several different owners over the years, including General Stephen D. Lee, Judge J.A. Orr and Jesse P. Woodward. The last owner was W.S. Lindamood, who bought the property in 1901. Lindamood spent several thousand dollars on improvements, including overhauling the plumbing and installing expensive grill work in several of the rooms. An old windmill erected in the yard enhanced its beauty. Lindamood was in the process of laying the hardwood floor when the house caught fire on May 5, 1909. Sparks from the kitchen are believed to have ignited the fire, although the rumor soon spread that it was set by a jealous housekeeper who was in love with Lindamood. Because the nearest hydrant was eight hundred feet away, the fire department could do little to save the house, which burned to the ground. Only two towering chimneys remained.

The financial loss on the house and furniture was estimated to be between $20,000 and $25,000; unfortunately, Lindamood carried only $5,000 insurance on the house and $1,000 on the furniture. Nevertheless,

Lindamood announced in an article published in the May 13, 1909 issue of the *Columbus Weekly Dispatch* that he intended to rebuild immediately: "He has not as yet decided the exact style of the house which he will erect, but it will be a modern house, in thorough keeping with the well-kept lot and its aristocratic environment." He was so determined not to be defeated by the loss of his frame mansion that he ordered that the work on the cement walks that were being laid around the original house continue.

Construction of Lindamood's new home, the Highland House, was completed in 1910. By the 2000s, the historically restored Greek Revival brick mansion was being operated as a bed-and-breakfast owned by Dr. James and Celeta Holzhauer. Mrs. Holzhauer readily admitted that something strange was going on inside her lavish home:

> *The piano plays by itself. I see and smell cigar smoke. It smells* [like a cherry blend]. *I have dolls that move and play tricks on me. I see images of spirits flowing up and down my stairs. Guests have been pushed down the front staircase. The basement is very scary. I refuse to go down to the basement because I was locked* [down there] *for over six hours until the basement door magically opened on its own.*

A paranormal investigation conducted by Jeff Harris, Dena Chunn, Fleur Harris and Dr. Mark Burtman gathered some fascinating evidence inside the old home. "The EMF readings were varied, and we found many 'hot spots,' including a large collection of old dolls that seem to have their own magnetic field," Harris said. The most fascinating photograph taken by the group was the image of a ghostly face in a mirror in the game room. Harris is convinced that he captured the face of a ghost in his photograph: "There is no picture of this person in that room. The only photo of this person is located on the floor below, and it has a large crack in the glass covering....We tried every angle shooting pictures and couldn't duplicate the effect." The investigators appear to have validated Mrs. Holzhauer's assertion that the house is "extremely haunted and active."

WISTERIA PLACE

Named for the old wisteria vine growing in the front yard, Wisteria House was built in 1854 at the cost of $7,000 for William R. Cameron, a planter

The ghost of William R. Cameron has been sighted walking past the kitchen window toward the back door of Wisteria Place.

from South Carolina who moved to Mississippi and embarked on a career as a successful legislator and state politician. Not only was he president of the Senate and president of the state Democratic Convention, but he also served as acting governor for a while. Some of the most notable southerners of the day were guests at Cameron's Greek Revival mansion, including General Nathan Bedford Forrest and Governor John Quitman. Unfortunately, Cameron lived only four years in the house before succumbing to typhoid fever shortly before his fifty-fourth birthday in 1858. Jefferson Davis, who was serving as the United States secretary of war, declared, "I have lost my best friend. Cameron was the purest, truest, noblest and best man I ever knew." Cameron's widow tried to rebuild her life by marrying another politician, Samuel Meek, several years later. However, tragedy visited the Cameron family once again with the deaths of William R. Cameron's two sons while fighting for the Confederacy with the Forty-third Mississippi Infantry, one at Chickamauga on September 1863 and the other at Jonesborough, Georgia, in August 1864.

Today, Wisteria Place is one of the most beautiful stops on Columbus's spring pilgrimage. The veranda is supported with six square, free-standing columns. The front façade is rendered even more majestic by the graceful balustrade on the balcony and the portico. The sidelights framing the doorway are made of cobalt, crimson and purple Bohemian glass. When the Camerons were entertaining, the jib windows were opened to make more room.

Wisteria Place is haunted by a ghost whose identity is unknown. Since the 1970s, the apparition of a man wearing a white shirt has been sighted walking briskly up the walkway past the kitchen window toward the back door. When family members opened the door, no one was standing outside. The owners, Mr. and Mrs. Harris Wallace, reported that individual family members had seen the ghost but that they had not discussed their paranormal encounters with one another. When they compared notes, they found similarities in their accounts that lent credence to their experiences. The frequency of the sightings, however, varied. Some family members said that the ghost appeared several times each week. Others said that months might pass before it showed up again.

Although three people died in Wisteria Place, locals believe that the specter is the ghost of William R. Cameron, who passed away in his bedroom in 1858, only four years after he moved in. Cameron's spirit seems to be trying to complete an urgent errand, the nature of which will probably never be revealed.

CALLOWAY HALL

The dormitory and administrative offices of the Columbus Female Institute were originally housed in a twelve-room antebellum mansion owned by Major Moore. The home was purchased by a group of concerned citizens in Columbus who believed that the city should offer higher education instruction for its young ladies. The school flourished until 1858, when a toy balloon set afloat by some mischievous young men landed on top of the beautiful white building and set the roof afire. The same group of citizens raised $30,000 for the construction of a new collegiate building called Old Main Dormitory. It was renamed thirty-three years later in honor of Mary J.S. Calloway, a former mathematics professor at the school. The new building housed three hundred students on three stories fronted by two porches located where the lobby stands today. The porches were replaced by a six-story tower. The school stayed open until the beginning of the Civil War. The Columbus Female Institute closed down for the duration of the war and was used as a field hospital. The dormitory reopened in 1867.

A despondent nurse named Mary is said to have hanged herself from the clock tower of Calloway Hall at the Mississippi University for Women.

In the 1860s and 1870s, social activist Sallie Reneau campaigned tirelessly for the creation of a state-funded, all-female university. Although she did secure approval for a women's institute of higher learning from the legislature, she could not persuade it to appropriate funding for the project. In 1884, the state legislature made history by voting to charter the first state-supported women's college in the United States. The mission of the Industrial Institute and College (II&C) was to provide intellectual training and vocational training for all women in the state. Many residents viewed the founding of the university as a boon for the "poor girls of Mississippi," who needed the means to support themselves. The City of Columbus donated the grounds and buildings of the old Columbus Female Institute (1847) to the state, as well as $50,000 in city bonds. The first 341 students enrolled in the II&C in October 1884. The school's name was changed to the Mississippi College for Women in 1920. The name was changed once again to Mississippi University for Women in 1974. The first male students were admitted eight years later. When Dr. Clyda Rent became president of "the W" in 1989, she was the first female executive officer of an institution of higher education in the state of Mississippi. Today, the W is renowned for its high-quality liberal arts instruction and for the ghost of Calloway Hall.

The most legendary part of Calloway Hall is the clock tower. The bell was installed soon after the building was constructed, but the clock was not installed until 1884, when the state took over the institution. The tower was remodeled for the placement of the clock according to the design of B.H. Bartlett of Des Moines, Iowa. His plan called for only a northern clock face, but a local citizen named Narrison Johnson paid to have smaller faces added to the east and west sides of the tower. The clock was wound every seven days. This system of ringing the bell was abandoned when electricity replaced the clock's winding operation. The massive pulleys, cables and weights were removed as well.

The twenty-four-inch bell is set in a carefully crafted wooden mount. For the first few decades of the university's existence, workers sounded the bell on the half hour and hour by pulling on a rope stretching through a hole from the tower to the basement. After several years, either the bell was disconnected from the clock or the clock ceased functioning. For the next few decades, the bell was sounded only on special occasions, like the signing of the Vietnam War Treaty in 1973 and the bicentennial in 1976. To ring the bell, a worker had to climb to the clapper and swing it by hand. Before the end of the decade, electricians led by Leroy Schoggen ran a line from the clapper to a motor. The bell was rung by pressing a button on the landing below. After the installation of the W's eleventh president, James Strobel, the clock was set to be running again. He also ordered the wooden clock faces to be replaced with Plexiglas panels. New gears and shafts running from the mechanism to the clock faces were installed as well. For years, the old clock faces and the worn steel rods were stored in the clock tower. The exterior spotlights that had been in place since 1934 were replaced with fluorescent tubes that illuminated the clock faces from the inside.

The old bell bears witness to the long history of the old school. On the side of the bell is inscribed, "Jones, Hitchcock and Col, Founders, 1857." On a plate in the bell's "green machine" are inscribed the words, "Seth Thomas, Aug. 15, 1885." The clapper strikes the bell from the north side 180 times every day. Over the years, the clapper has worn a smooth space on the exterior the bell. The clapper itself is flattened out on the end.

Calloway Hall was renovated twice between 1920 and 1976. In 1938, South Calloway Hall was added. For a time, it was used as the library. The old dorm was renovated a second time in 1968, when the interior was completely rebuilt using steel beams. On October 10, 1992, a tornado that ripped through Columbus removed the top of the tower and destroyed the clock. Architect Robert Parker Adams of Jackson was hired to restore the tower to its original appearance. The project was financed with state and federal funding.

According to local paranormal groups, these changes in the original building could have stirred up its resident spirit. The ghost stories originated on the fourth floor, which was closed in 1966. Except for those rare occasions when the elevator inexplicably opens on the fourth floor, the hall is accessible only from a third-floor stairway, which ends at a locked door. Generations of students have trudged up the twenty-two stairs in the hope of catching a glimpse of the tower's ghost through the window of the door. Many of these "intrepid" students who ventured up the stairs chalked their names on the tower walls. Names like "Grace Williams 1934–1935" and "Babe-o-Buck 1951" are still visible.

The ghost story of Calloway Hall has evolved into several different variants. According to one, a young lady who found herself "in trouble" flung her clothes from the tower window and hanged herself. In another version, the suicide victim was a male student. The oldest ghost story dates back to the Civil War. Following the Battle of Shiloh, a large number of wounded soldiers were brought to Columbus, where they were cared for in private homes and in Calloway Hall. The story goes that a volunteer nurse named Mary fell in love with one of the wounded soldiers. A romance blossomed. Invigorated perhaps by the love he felt for the young woman, the soldier recuperated quickly. Shortly after the couple became engaged, the soldier rejoined his unit. While waiting for him to return, Mary threw herself into her work, doing her part to alleviate the pain and misery of her patients. One day, she received the sad news that her lover had become a casualty of war. Driven mad by grief, she climbed the stairs to the top of the tower, where she tied a noose around her neck and jumped to her death.

Stories about the ghost of Mary the nurse surfaced in the twentieth century. Mary is reputed to be a mischievous ghost who announces her presence by piling books in the middle of dorm room floors during the night or by turning up the volume on the stereos as the girls are listening to the music. Sometimes, Mary's mournful side takes audible form. Some students claim to have heard moaning and crying coming from the fourth floor.

At least two people say they have seen the ghost. In his book *Haunted Halls of Ivy*, Daniel W. Barefoot tells the story of a painter who was working in Columbus Hall, which is attached to Calloway Hall. At the end of the day, he chained and locked the front door. As he was driving away, he saw the figure of a woman wearing a Victorian-era dress open the front door of Columbus Hall and walk inside. Astounded by what he had just seen, the painter drove back to Columbus Hall. The door was chained and locked, just as he had left it.

Barefoot tells another story about a young lady who was sleeping in her room in Calloway Hall when she was awakened by the feeling that she was not alone. She woke up and turned on the light, but no one was there. As she was lying back down, she noticed an indentation in the mattress. It seemed as if someone had been sitting there, watching her. After a few restless minutes, she overcame her fear and fell back asleep. A few minutes later, she felt icy fingers caressing her face. When she opened her eyes, she saw a white shape hovering over her bed. The terrified girl screamed, and the apparition vanished.

Kenny Reynolds, who attended the Mississippi School of Math and Science at the W during the summer of 1995, also had his own harrowing experience with the ghost of Mary:

> *I've heard that Mary is still waiting for her soldier on the fourth floor. I'd also heard that the elevators would automatically go up to the fourth floor, even though nobody sent them up there, and that the clock occasionally strikes thirteen times at midnight instead of twelve. I thought I heard it chime thirteen times one day, but I was half asleep, so I might have miscounted. One time I was visiting [my friends] Misty Holcomb and Stacey Jemison on the third floor, and I heard someone walking around on the fourth floor. It's hard to say exactly what the sound was. It was just general bumps in the area. It happened about three o'clock in the afternoon on a Friday in late August. I asked them what it could possibly be, and they said, nonchalantly, "Oh, it's just the ghost."*

Misty Holcomb gave Kenny her own version of the hauntings on the fourth floor:

> *If the elevator takes you to the fourth floor—and it's not supposed to—it's the ghost of the nurse who does this. When the door opens, there she is. You can hear her moving chairs around up there. If you don't know the ghost story and you are on the fourth floor, you scream and run away. It's very spooky.*

World War II produced its own Calloway ghost story. A young pilot who was engaged to a female student at the W was killed in a fiery plane crash. His fiancée was so grief-stricken that she left behind a trunk of clothes and love letters and went home. In another version of the story, the girl ended her life by jumping off the clock tower. A discovery made in the 1950s lends some credence to the tale of the despondent war widow. A workman discovered a small trunk with rusty hinges. He pried open the trunk and found some mildewed clothes and a diary belonging to Ann Grimes, a 1942 graduate of the W. Members of the Alumnae Association and editors of the school newspaper, *The Spectator*, solved the mystery. Ann Elizabeth Grimes fell in love with A.L. Lane, an officer stationed in Columbus. After graduating, she served as a social adviser for the university for one year. The couple was married at the First Method Church in Columbus. Soon afterward, Lane was deployed overseas, where he was killed in a plane crash. In a letter written to alumnae secretary Marcie Sanders concerning a class reunion in 1972, Lane's widow said that she had remarried and was now Mrs. Bryon A. Huribut of Twin Falls, Idaho. A few students and staff were disappointed to learn that sometimes ghost stories are just that: stories.

"THREE-LEGGED LADY ROAD"

Haunted roads are a motif commonly found in American ghost lore. Ghost sightings and a hell hound have been reported on Clinton Road in West Milford, Passaic County, New Jersey. The ghost stories centered on Bloodspoint Road in Boone County, Illinois, have been generated by such violent occurrences as murders, accidents and suicides. The spectral shapes of Confederate soldiers and American Indians have been sighted on Zombie Road in St. Louis, Missouri. Without a doubt, the most legendary road in the Golden Triangle is "Three-Legged Lady Road" in Columbus.

The haunted section of Nash Road stretches from the ruins of a church to an unnamed bridge. A number of legends about the haunting of Nash Road have been passed down over the years. According to one of the variants, a young woman named Rose was captured by a Satanic cult that conducted its ceremonies on Nash Road. The devil worshipers cut her body into pieces and scattered them throughout the woods. The unquiet spirits of the girl and her despondent mother walk the road to this day. Some say that the despondent woman carries the only body part she could find—one of the girl's amputated legs—under her arm, giving the witnesses the impression that she has three legs. Others claim that the mother sewed Rose's leg to her own body so the pair would always be together.

Nash Road is also known as "Three-Legged Lady Road" because of the apparition of a woman who races people who challenge her by flashing their lights and honking their horns three times. *Courtesy Marilyn Brown.*

In another version of the tale, a farmer's wife fell in love with a Civil War veteran. The pair conducted their clandestine affair while her husband worked in the fields. One day, her husband found out about his wife's infidelity and, in a fit of rage, killed her lover. He dragged the man's corpse down Nash Road, and as he was making his way over the bridge, a leg was torn off the man's body. When the woman learned of her lover's death, she became mad with grief. After the veteran's funeral, she sewed her lover's leg onto her own body. A few weeks later, she murdered her husband and then turned the gun on herself. The woman's ghost floats from her farmhouse on Nash Road to the church where her lover's funeral was held. In a variant of this tale, the farm wife loved her husband, but her love turned to rage when she discovered that he had a woman on the side. She killed him, dismembered the corpse and sewed his leg onto her body.

These are only two versions of the Three-Legged Lady Road tale that are still told in Columbus. Despite their differences, all of the stories end the same way. People wishing to meet the ghost of Nash Road must drive to the old church late at night and flash their lights off and on and honk their horns three times. The Three-Legged Lady announces her appearance by knocking on the roof of the car. This gesture initiates a race between the car and the apparition, which has an "edge" because of her third leg. Throughout the entirety of the race, she slams her body into the side of the car. When the driver reaches the end of the road, the Three-Legged Lady vanishes.

This story is a good example of an urban legend, which folklorist Jan Harold Brunvand defined as "highly captivating and plausible, but mainly fictional, oral narratives that are widely told as true stories." Stories like this one are kept alive by people who have had personal experiences that prove their veracity. A simple Google search of "Three-Legged Lady Road in Columbus, Mississippi," will produces dozens of encounters with a three-legged specter that chases drivers along Nash Road late at night, leaving a record of the encounters with scratches, dents or handprints on the cars. A ghost light, which has been described as an orb and a floating lantern, has been sighted on the road. Nash Road really exists, but the church is gone; only the concrete slab remains. Anyone interested in meeting the Three-Legged Lady should know that Nash Road is a narrow, dirt-and-gravel road, parts of which are under water some of the time.

ARMSTRONG ROAD

Another urban legend from Mississippi's Golden Triangle is the ghost of the railroad tracks on Armstrong Road in Columbus. In the standard version of the tale, a young woman walked to the railroad tracks to await the arrival of her husband immediately following the end of the Civil War. She stood at the tracks for several hours before being told by a neighbor that her husband was killed in a train accident. With tears in her eyes, the woman insisted that her neighbor was mistaken. Her husband was not dead. His train was late, that was all. Every day after receiving the news of her husband's demise, the bereaved wife continued her daily walk up and down the tracks with lantern in hand, looking for her husband. One day, the woman accepted the fact that her husband really was dead and that she would never see him again. Reluctant to live with the sad truth, she waited for a train to come barreling down the tracks and calmly stepped in front of it. She was killed instantly.

A number of reports regarding the ghostly activity at the railroad tracks have been made over the years. Some witnesses swear that they saw the spectral form of a woman walking down the railroad tracks. Some curiosity

The ghost of a woman carrying a lantern has been seen walking down the railroad tracks at the Armstrong Road Crossing.

seekers who ventured to the site at night swear that they saw the light from a lantern moving along the tracks. In most of these stories, the light emitted from the lantern is multicolored.

Not surprisingly, the tragic tale of the war widow has become the basis for a rite of passage among the young people of Columbus. The story goes that if you stop on the tracks, flash your lights off and on three times and honk your horn three times, the woman's lantern will suddenly appear in the distance and move at a very high rate of speed toward your car. The logic behind this seemingly meaningless ritual is that the woman's ghost assumes the car's headlights are the train's headlights. Desperate to be reunited with her husband, her spirit races down the tracks toward the car.

Of course, rational explanations can be given for most of the mysterious occurrences at the railroad tracks. Drivers could actually be seeing the headlights of a car moving across the tracks at another crossing. The ghost light could also be the glare of a streetlight partially obscured by trees. Regardless of the reason for the phenomenon, people should definitely refrain from parking on the railroad tracks at Armstrong Road.

THE LEGEND OF BLACK CREEK

Stories of the headless horseman are embedded in European culture. Irish folklore speaks of a headless fairy called a "dullahan" that holds his head up high while riding a black horse. In Scotland, people speak of the headless ghost of a warrior named Ewan who was decapitated at a clan battle at Glen Cainnir. The Brothers Grimm included two German folktales of headless horsemen in their collection. The most famous headless horseman tale written in America is Washington Irving's "The Legend of Sleepy Hollow." Chances are good that Irving read the journal of the American general William Heath, who wrote of the decapitation of a Hessian soldier by a cannonball at the Battle of Merritt Hill in White Plains, New York. Interestingly enough, Columbus has its own version of the headless horseman legend.

Joseph B. Cobb published his version of Columbus's headless horseman tale in his book *Mississippi Scenes* (1851). His story focuses on a man named Tony Randall, who worked on farms in and around Simstown. He particularly enjoyed singing hymns as he performed his chores. One of the farmers who employed gave him the job of delivering his produce to the market in Columbus. As a rule, Randall was accompanied by an old slave named Uncle Ned when he went on these trips. On his way to Columbus, Tony had to ford Black Creek, which was rumored to be haunted by the ghosts of two of Andrew Jackson's dragoons, a Choctaw Indian and a murderer who reenacted his crime every year on the anniversary of the murder. Both men were highly superstitious and, therefore, reluctant to go anywhere near Black Creek.

One night, Randall and Uncle Ned were about to ford Black Creek on their return trip from Columbus. Randall tried to quicken the pace of the mules, but they insisted on stopping at the creek to take a drink of water. While Randall and Uncle Ned were riding, their imaginations were fueled by such strange sounds as a clanging noise, a low whistle from the slope of the hill and the pounding hoof beats of a horse. As a barrage of fireballs flew over his head, Randall witnessed the reenactment of the murderer of a traveler and the ghosts of two dragoons. He also heard a human body plunge into the dark waters of the creek. The mules, just as terrified as the two men, reared up, throwing Randall into the back of the wagon. The animals galloped down the road, desperate to return to the safety of their stalls in Simstown. The next morning, passersby discover the wreckage and Uncle Ned, clearly inebriated, lying on the ground. Tony Randall was never seen again.

Cobb obviously embellished the local legend with elements "borrowed" from Irving's short story. Irving's main characters have their counterparts in Cobb's tale: Ichabod Crane (Tony Randall), Bram Bones (Bob Bagshot) and Katrina van Tassell (Charity Plainlove). "The Legend of Black Creek" seems to have almost everything Irving's story has except for the headless horseman.

THE GHOSTLY DRAGOONS OF MILITARY ROAD

In 1812, a network of roads was constructed to enable General Andrew Jackson's army to move quickly to the Gulf ports of New Orleans, Biloxi, Mobile and Pensacola in the event of an attack by the British. On April 24, 1816, Congress appropriated $10,000 for the repair and maintenance of the road from Columbia, Tennessee, to Madisonville, Louisiana, and the road between Fort Hawkins and Fort Stoddard. Andrew Jackson, who at the time was the commander of the Army District at Nashville, was officially in charge of the entire construction. The First and Eighth Infantries supplied some of the labor, but most of the construction was done by Jackson's subordinates. Captain H. Young, who surveyed the route, completed the job in June 1817. His survey indicated the places where bridges were needed, so Congress allocated an addition $5,000. In April 1819, Major Perrin Will was placed in command of the fifty-man construction gang. When the road was completed in May 1820, it stretched at its longest point 516 miles from Nashville to New Orleans. All totaled, the construction gangs consisted of three hundred men, including blacksmiths, sawyers and carpenters. The road included twenty thousand feet of causeway through the swamps of Noxubee County, Mississippi, and thirty-five bridges. Over the next three decades, much of the traffic that had been moving on the Natchez Trace was diverted to Andrew Jackson's Military Road. Some people even built their homes along the new road. By 1845, Robinson Road had replaced Andrew Jackson's Military Road as the primary pathway for settlers.

At one time, Andrew Jackson's Military Road crossed the Tombigbee River in Columbus. Part of the road also crossed Black Creek. In his book *Mississippi Scenes*, Joseph B. Cobb described the Black Creek crossing as "a forbidding spot, shaded by huge willow trees and swamp oaks, whose thick foliage imparts an aspect of gloom and terror, sufficiently ominous to put a suspicious soul on his guard." This area's violent past was preserved in a number of local legends, including the tale of a young Native American brave who murdered his brother, tied a bundle of large rocks to his body and threw him in Black Creek. A number of people are believed to have drowned in the flooded creek. Many travelers were assaulted, robbed and even murdered at the crossing. Looking at the crossing today, one would hardly guess that it was the scene of so much suffering. The road has been straightened out, and what was once a very foreboding region is now a residential area.

The tragic incident that seems to have left the most indelible imprint on this stretch of Andrew Jackson's Military Road occurred in 1817. In Cobb's account, Andrew Jackson arrived at the crossing during a spring flood. Eager to ford the creek, he ordered two young dragoons to wade into the water and check the water's depth. The hapless dragoons were caught up in the current and swept away. Their bodies were never recovered. The story goes that on dark, cloudy nights, the apparitions of the dead dragoons can be seen on horseback wearing plumes in their hats. Large, wicked-looking swords hang from their sides. Cobb wrote that the horses "rear[ed] and plung[ed] through the air about the height that the creek usually rises to a high flood, whilst a great white figure [darts] up suddenly with a shriek out of the dark pool and then [falls] back heavily again, as if pulled with a dead weight."

This legend raises an important question: did this tragic incident really occur? History tells us that Andrew Jackson did not travel this part of his Military Road. However, in an article published in the *Starkville Dispatch* on October 24, 2010, columnist Rufus Ward says, "Not far north of Black Creek on a hill overlooking Howard Creek is a ca. 1817 grave of a U.S. soldier who died during the construction of the Military Road." No one knows for sure how many men gave their lives while building Andrew Jackson's Military Road. It stands to reason, then, that the drowned dragoons in Cobb's legend could have been two of the nameless men who died trying to make Andrew Jackson's dream road a reality.

THE AMZI LOVE HOUSE

Amzi Love was eight years old when he came to Columbus in about 1830. His family came from Chester County, South Carolina. Before moving to South Carolina, they had emigrated from the Isle of Skye, Scotland. Before that, they came from North Antrum County, Ireland, which is the most

The Amzi Love House was built in 1848 in the Greek Revival and Gothic Revival architectural styles.

northern county in Ireland. The family lived in Scotland and Ireland for two hundred years before coming to the United States in 1750.

The Amzi Love Home at 305 Seventh Street is a seven-bedroom Italianate cottage built by a local contractor named James Lull in 1848. However, the house is also a good example of an architectural style that has come to be known as "Columbus Eclectic." The Gothic influence can be seen in the arches on the front porch. The Greek Revival influence is evident in the little cutouts above the doors and windows. It has two bedrooms on the lower floor and two bedrooms on the upper floor. The ceilings are twelve and a half feet high. Amzi's father owned this entire block at one time. The Amzi Love House has been in the family for seven generations. Sid Carradine is the first man to occupy the house in one hundred years:

Amzi Love is my great-great grandfather. It's a nickname for Amiziah. He's named after King Amiziah. He built this house in 1848 for his bride, Edith Wallace. It was a honeymoon gift that he surprised her with after they got married. She was from Alabama. Before they were married, they were in a horse-drawn carriage, and as they were passing this house that was being built for him, he told her it belonged to his sister and her husband. Amzi grew up two doors down in a house that his father built. Amzi had an older brother, a younger brother and four sisters. So Amzi was taking his bride to meet his sisters. After they got married, Edith was surprised.

Amzi Love became a lawyer. He was elected to the circuit court. He was also a thirty-second-degree Mason. According to Sid Carradine, Amzi took the most pride in being president of his men's Presbyterian Sunday school class.

Amzi and his Edith had five girls and one boy, all of whom were born in the Amzi Love House. The last-born child, Annie, was the only one to have children. She had three of them. All of the girls graduated from the Columbus Female Institute. Edith Love died of yellow fever in 1872. Amzi's mother helped him with the children while he went by riverboat to Memphis on business trips. He died of yellow fever two years later. Left to fend for themselves, the sisters were told by the "carpetbaggers" who were running the town that they had to put up a $5,000 guardian bond in order to keep the house. To raise money, the girls made bedspreads and rugs, taught school and gave guitar and violin lessons, reading lessons, Latin lessons and French lessons. Through their hard work, they finally made enough money to save their home.

Mattie Love, the youngest daughter, died in 1951. She was an artist who painted a picture based on Thomas Gray's poem "Elegy in a Country Churchyard" when she was sixteen years old. She entered the painting in an art show in Vicksburg in 1870 and won a silver tray. The painting and the silver tray are on display in the enclosed porch, along with crimping irons, jelly pots and ice cream molds. Mattie built the cottage next door to the Amzi Love Home as an art studio in 1885.

Annie Love had three children. After her husband left, she moved back into the Amzi Love House. Annie's daughter, Gladys, wanted to be an artist like her aunt, so she took art lessons from Mattie at her studio next door. Gladys earned a fine arts degree from the W and taught at Franklin Academy, the first free public school in Mississippi. Some of Gladys's art students were sent to Europe during World War I to help wounded soldiers in hospitals regain the use of their hands by painting pictures of ships, trees and other objects.

The furniture dates from the 1830s to the 1890s. Some pieces came from Amzi's father's house. Amzi and Edith added other piece of furniture later. The door is bordered by sidelights. The transom is composed of diamond-shaped glass panes. In the entrance hall stands the unsupported cantilevered walnut staircase with two beautiful newel posts. "This is a middle-class cottage. If Amzi hadn't had the front porch and the extra money for the Venetian glass and decorative wood carvings, it would be just a clapboard house," Sid said. The baby carriage sitting next to the staircase belonged to the daughters. It was pulled around the yard by a pet goat. Ladies who came calling in the afternoons to pay their respects placed their cards in a calling card dish in the entranceway. All of the lamp fixtures have been rewired. On exhibit in the two Empire secretaries in the parlor are Mrs. Love's wedding band, Amzi's pocket watch, the five silver thimbles belonging to the five daughters, several dolls made during the Civil War, a pewter inkwell and a piece of hair jewelry made from the daughters' hair.

The kitchen was originally detached from the house. It became part of the house around 1920. The back porch was enclosed at this time as well. Outside of the house, the dairy and smokehouse are still standing.

In addition to the paintings, letters, knitting, dresses, quilts and antiques, the Amzi Love Home also contains a ghost. According to Sid Carrington, a neighbor named Jason Robinson was walking his dog down the street:

> *Jason, who's a paleontologist, said, "Sid, my dog stopped walking. I looked up and saw a transparent woman dressed in a Victorian outfit. She went through the door of your house and through your station wagon. She floated around the smokehouse and the magnolia tree and then went next door to the Lincoln House."' Jason stood there looking, and a policeman came by and said, "Jason, are you all right? Have you been drinking?" Jason replied, "I haven't had a drink, I haven't had a smoke, I haven't had anything." The dog was growling, and the policeman said, "What's wrong?" Jason replied, "You won't believe it, but I just saw a ghost come out of Sid's kitchen."*

After Jason calmed down, he told Sid that the bluish-white figure resembled a lamp shade, narrow at the top and broad at the bottom. She was wearing a large hat and a lacy dress that revealed her bare arms. Jason could just make out the woman's prominent nose and her eyes. In his opinion, she bore an uncanny resemblance to Sid's mother. Following his sighting of the female specter, Jason and his dog always avoided the Amzi House on their daily walks.

Although Sid was intrigued by Jason's story, he was not really surprised. Soon after he moved into the Amzi Love House, he began hearing noises coming from the second floor. He suspects that the spectral woman might be his great-aunt Edith, who broke her hip while visiting Memphis and was

The ghostly figure of a woman was sighted drifting through the kitchen door of the Amzi Love House and passing through the wall of the Lincoln Home next door.

never able to revisit the Amzi Love Home. Sid thinks his great-aunt wants to spend eternity in the old house that meant so much to her when she was alive. He also believes she is the spirit haunting his home because she was a tall woman, and several of the witnesses who have seen the ghost have described her as being above average height.

Back in the early 2000s, a visitor verified Sid's belief that the Amzi Love House was haunted. At the end of the tour, he was standing in the Amzi Love Room and said, "I feel the spirits, and there's a ghost in here." The visitor's apparent sensitivity to the presence of spirits seems to lend credence to the various sightings over the years.

HOLLYHOCKS

In the late nineteenth century, five mercantile buildings ran an entire block on Fifth Street. Known as the "Merchant's Block," the buildings were developed

The building in which the Hollyhocks Gift Shop is housed is haunted by what owner Herriott calls a "trickster ghost." *Courtesy Gail Reynolds.*

in 1882 by a group of investors. They were connected by a balcony on the second floor. A mercantile took up the ground floor. Hollyhocks Gift Shop is now housed in the last of the original buildings. When the building was completed in 1882, it was called the Mercantile Building. It is now called the Herriott Building. Over the years, the building has been the site of a number of businesses, including the Gunter Brothers Funeral Parlor in the 1920s and Hardin Radio and Appliance in the 1960s.

The owner of Hollyhocks, Gloria Herriott, says that it is the most photographed building in Columbus because of the paintings on the end of the building:

> *No one knew that they were there until the building that stood right next to it burned down in the 1980s. They have been preserved by that building all these years. The painted advertisements are now starting to fade away. We can't preserve the paintings because they are lead based. I would like to repaint the advertisements after the originals are gone. For now, we and everyone else are enjoying them. People stand in the little park next to us and take pictures of the building all the time.*

These painted advertisements were discovered on the exterior wall of the Hollyhocks Gift Shop after the old building next door burned down. *Courtesy Gail Reynolds.*

The Herriott Building is the second historic building restored by the Herriotts. "When we bought the building in 2006, the balcony was in pretty bad shape. We completely restored the balcony," Gloria said. "We took a couple of the original wrought-iron grills that were being used to keep the doors shut and sent them to a foundry in Birmingham. The foundry used the grills to make molds. The grills that are on the balcony now were made from those molds."

Maurice and Gloria Herriott made extensive renovations on the interior of the building as well. "The interior was in pretty bad shape because there had been a fire there at one time," Gloria said. "The second floor needed a lot of work as well. Several businesses were located on the ground floor, but the second floor was abandoned after the cotton merchants left. We found a number of documents relating to the cotton business when we were cleaning up."

While the workers were reinforcing the walls of the third floor to convert it into a living space for Maurice and Gloria, they made a startling discovery:

> One of the workers told me that they had found a body up there. I climbed up the stairs and peeked over the edge. Lying prone on the floor was a skeleton. It was not a medical skeleton. It looked as if someone had fallen on the floor and died. It is also possible that the corpse was placed on the floor. I don't know what happened to the skeleton. I've been unable to find out the identity of the person.

Gloria seems to think that the "trickster ghost" that haunts the building might be the spirit of the man who died there. The ghost seems to be most active in the basement, which was used as a morgue at one time:

> He moves things in the basement all the time. My husband makes crystals. Sometimes, we will find that a crystal has been moved to an entirely different place during the night. The girls who work for me have heard things drop onto the floor of the basement. When they check it out, they find that nothing has fallen. So far, we haven't actually seen the ghost that is doing these things.

One of the construction workers who erected the building in the 1880s could also be "hanging around." The signature of one of these men and a date have been carved into one of the beams in the basement. Perhaps the attachment he felt for the structure he helped build has extended into the afterlife.

Gloria's husband, Maurice, believes there is a definite connection between the paranormal activity in the basement and the funeral home. "When we first got here, the basement had just a dirt floor," Maurice said.

> *There was a pit in the floor, and I was told that the owners of the old funeral home threw unclaimed bodies in there and burned them up with acid. Sometimes, random things disappear, and I never find them. One time, I placed something in a hard-to-reach spot, and it disappeared. The girls who work here sometimes hear noises when they come down to the basement.*

Despite the strange things that occur in the basement, Maurice said that he and Gloria are never afraid down there: "In fact, sometimes I come down here to read for the peace and quiet."

Gloria Herriott is not really frightened by the entity that sometimes disrupts her regular routine inside the old building. "I'm glad to say it's a friendly ghost," Gloria said. "He doesn't really bother us. In fact, I think he likes us."

THE STEPHEN D. LEE HOME

The Stephen D. Lee Home at 316 Seventh Street North was built in the Italianate style by Major Thomas Garton Blewett. Born in North Carolina in 1798, Blewitt made his living as an engineer and as a planter. He married Regina De Graffenried in 1815. He moved his wife and children to Columbus in 1832. Major Blewitt and his wife suffered two painful blows while living in the house. Their youngest daughter, Amy, died in the house in 1854. Their younger son, Randle, was killed at the Battle of Seven Pines in 1862. Following Major Blewitt's death in 1871, their widowed daughter, Regina, inherited the home. She passed the house down to her two daughters, Mary Harrison and Regina Lily Harrison Lee, who was married to Confederate general Stephen D. Lee.

General Lee is remembered in Columbus as a soldier, writer, educator and politician. Born in Charleston, South Carolina, on September 22, 1833, Lee was distantly related to Robert E. Lee. He was enrolled in West Point at age seventeen. When he graduated in 1854, one of the members of his class was J.E.B. Stuart. After receiving his commission in the U.S. Army as a second lieutenant, Lee was deployed to Kansas, Texas and Florida. He

The Stephen D. Lee Home was built by Major Thomas G. Blewitt between 1844 and 1847.

resigned his commission in December 1860, when South Carolina seceded from the Union. He immediately enlisted in the Confederate army, where he served as aide-de-camp to General P.G.T. Beauregard at Charleston Harbor. While there, Lee delivered the terms of surrender to Major Robert Anderson, commander of Fort Sumter. He then served as an artillery officer for the Army of Northern Virginia. President Jefferson Davis commended his bravery at the Battle of Second Manassas. Following his promotion to colonel, Lee distinguished himself at the Battle of Antietam by helping repel General Burnside's army across Stone Bridge. He was promoted to the rank of brigadier general and transferred to Mississippi to aid in the defense of Vicksburg. Lee was wounded in the shoulder in the Battle of Champion's Hill and was taken prisoner in July 1863 after Vicksburg was occupied by the Union army. Lee was released in a prisoner exchange on October 3, 1863. He was promoted to major general and placed in command of cavalry in Alabama, Mississippi, western Tennessee and eastern Louisiana. One of his subordinate generals was General Nathan Bedford Forrest, who fought alongside Lee and thwarted a raid by the Union army at the Battle of Tupelo on July 14–15, 1864. Lee, who had been promoted to the rank of

Confederate general Stephen D. Lee married Regina Lily, Major Blewett's granddaughter, and lived in the house until his death in 1905.

lieutenant general in June, participated in the Battles of Franklin and Nashville. While leading a rear guard action, Lee was wounded once again.

At war's end, Lee came to Columbus and moved into Major Blewitt's former home with his wife, Regina Lily Harrison Lee. He devoted much of the remainder of his life to civic affairs. Lee was instrumental in the creation of Vicksburg National Military Park. His abiding interest in history led him to become president of the board of trustees of the Mississippi Department of Archives & History. Because of Lee's concern for Confederate veterans, he helped found the UCV (United Confederate Veterans) and its successor, the SCV (Sons of Confederate Veterans). He also made important contributions to education in Mississippi, becoming the first president of Mississippi A&M, the precursor of Mississippi State University. On May 29, 1908, Lee died in Vicksburg.

Mary Harrison inherited the Lees' home following their deaths. In 1909, the house received its most illustrious guest, President William Howard Taft, who was visiting Columbus. Mary lived in the house until she died in 1916, when the Lees' only child, Blewett Lee, sold the entire block the house was located on to the Columbus School Board, which built Stephen D. Lee High School on the south side of the house. The wings of the Stephen D. Lee House were removed when it was converted into a home economics building and cafeteria. The high school was completely destroyed by fire in 1959, but the Stephen D. Lee Home suffered only minor damage. In 1971, the Stephen D. Lee Home and Museum was listed on the National Register of Historic Places.

Accounts of paranormal activity inside the Stephen D. Lee Home surfaced in the late 1980s. At this time, a young couple was serving as caretakers of the home. Immediately, they noticed that something about the old house was not "quite right." They began hearing weird sounds late at night. Lights switched on and off by themselves. They lived in the house for only a few months before moving out. The next couple who moved in had no knowledge of the previous tenants' strange experiences. They did not report anything out of the ordinary taking place during their stay.

In 1992, Carolyn Kaye became the new curator of the Stephen D. Lee Home. She and her husband began hearing things right after they moved in. While she was unpacking in their apartment on their first day in the house, she heard the back door open and slam shut, as if someone had rushed inside the house. A few minutes later, she heard someone walking up the stairs. She walked out of the apartment and looked around, but no one was there. As she was standing there, she felt a blast of warm air. A few minutes later, her husband entered the house and walked up the stairs. Carolyn resisted the temptation to tell him what had happened because she knew he would try to find a logical explanation. At the time, he did not believe in ghosts.

Her husband's attitude toward the paranormal began to change the next morning. He told Carolyn that he had had a sleepless night because of all the coughing. Carolyn told him that she did not remember coughing during the night. Her husband replied, "It wasn't you. It was coming from the next room."

The paranormal activity escalated over the next few weeks. The couple heard other unsettling noises, like phantom footsteps and the crashing sound of a large tray falling to the floor. The spirits in the house manifested themselves through smell as well. Once in a while, the sweet smell of lilies wafted through the house.

One month after moving into the Stephen D. Lee Home, Carolyn was giving a tour to a group of tourists. At the end of the tour when people were leaving the house, two ladies stayed behind. One of them pointed to a chair in the parlor and said, "Tell me about that." Carolyn assumed that the woman wanted to know why this style of chair was in the same room with furniture from another period. Carolyn had just begun her explanation when the woman interrupted her. "No, no," the woman said. "Tell me about the lady sitting in the chair." Not knowing what to say, Carolyn replied that the ghost must be the spirit of Mary Harrison, the last family member to live in the house.

A young girl standing in the parlor at Christmastime saw the apparition of a woman wearing a white dress and diamonds.

The identity of the ghost became clearer during Carolyn's first Christmas in the home. Her children and grandchildren came to the home on Christmas morning to experience Christmas in a Victorian atmosphere. The children were busy opening their presents when Carolyn's five-year-old granddaughter suddenly stopped what she was doing. She stood up and stared into a corner of the room. Carolyn asked her what she was looking at, and the child replied that she saw a pretty lady standing there, looking at her. The lady was smiling, and she "sparkled with lots of diamonds. Her feet were not touching the floor."

Carolyn suspected that the girl might have seen the spirit of Lily Lee, whose portrait hangs in the parlor. Her suspicions were confirmed in the spring. One day while Carolyn was doing spring cleaning, she decided to take down the curtains so they could be washed and ironed. She was looking at the windows when she discovered the name "Lily" etched into one of the panes. Carolyn was amazed by her discovery because the etching had not been there when she washed the windows in the fall. She did some research and found no record of anyone else having etched the name on the window.

The most extraordinary thing about the etching was that she could not feel the scratches in the glass when she ran her fingers over the name inside or outside the house.

Carolyn's mind then went back to her first few weeks in the Stephen D. Lee Home, when she experienced periods of melancholy. Sometimes when she was really "down," she felt a ghostly finger touch her cheek. At other times, she was certain someone had caressed her stomach. She realized that this caring, sympathetic entity was probably the spirit of Lily.

Lily made her presence known in other ways over the next few months. The curator's bed is always made up before tours. One day before the tour began, Carolyn walked into the room and was surprised to find the indentation of a person lying in the bed. On another occasion, Carolyn was cleaning the rugs when, all at once, she heard a ghostly "sneeze." She turned and noticed dust flying in the direction of the sneeze. Carolyn concluded that Lily was watching her work and got a nose full of dust. One day, Carolyn received a phone call from a woman who had attended a wedding in the Stephen D. Lee Home the night before. In a nervous voice, she told Carolyn that she saw the spectral image of a woman standing on the staircase. Several times when Carolyn and her husband were out of the house, people passing by the home have seen the figure of a woman standing in the bedroom window.

As a rule, people who have seen Lily's ghost describe her as she appears in her portrait, with brown hair piled on top of her head and wearing a white dress. However, Gary Lancaster, the assistant manager of the house, has seen Lily many times, and his description of her is far different from those of most witnesses. As a rule, she appears to him as a reflection in the mirror wearing a pink dress with her hair down. Gary believes Lily has a strong attachment to the house because she spent most of her life there. She finally died of a protracted illness inside the house she loved so much.

The second ghost that haunts the old house is believed to be the spirit of Lily's sister, Mary. Witnesses describe her as an elderly lady wearing a blue-gray Victorian dress. Some people, including Carolyn, have caught sight of the tail of her dress almost floating down the stairs. Gary Lancaster has seen her standing in the parlor. Carolyn had a rather humorous encounter with Mary's ghost one day when she was giving a tour. The visitors were shocked to learn that the lady they had seen wearing a Victorian dress was not one of the docents.

The third ghost haunts the Florence McLeod Hazard Museum on the second floor. This particular spirit is heard, not seen. This ghost is thought to be the spirit of a little girl. Carolyn's sister and children have heard piano

Lily's ghost is believed to have etched her name on a pane of glass in the Stephen D. Lee Home.

music echoing through the halls, even though there is no piano up there. One wonders if residual energy clinging to some of the artifacts on display on the second floor is responsible for the eerie sounds.

The most mysterious presence in the house is known only as the "shadow man." This dark specter has been seen moving from the parlor to the dining room, where it exits the house through a window. Both Carolyn and Gary have seen this shadow person.

The fifth ghost is the spirit of Major Thomas G. Blewett. His ghost has been sighted by Gary and by Carolyn's granddaughter, who claims to have spoken to the major. Even as an adult, she can recall the conversations she had with him. Other children have seen the ghost as well. In 1997, several ladies who were preparing for a reception inside the house noticed Carolyn's granddaughter, a toddler at the time, playing "peek-a-boo" with someone who resembled the older gentleman in the portrait. Clearly, the major enjoys the company of children, and they like being around him as well.

Hundreds of people visit the Stephen D. Lee Home every year. The historic building is a favorite stop on the Pilgrimage of Homes tour. The elegant mansion has become a popular venue for receptions of all kinds, including wedding receptions. However, sometimes the spirits that haunt the Stephen D. Lee Home seem compelled to make it known that this is their house and always will be.

ERROLLTON

William B. Weaver, of Columbus, built Errolton in 1848. The two-story home is constructed of the finest building materials. Select lumber was shipped from Mobile. Weaver had the marble mantels imported from Italy. At the time, it was one of the most beautiful homes in town. Errolton exhibits elements of the Greek Revival, Italianate and Gothic Revival architectural styles. The house is fronted by a Greek Revival doorway, complete with pilasters and dentils. The sidelights and transom lights are made of red glass to warm the northern side of the house. Blue glass was used in the rear entrance to cool the sunlight from the southern side. The Greek Revival influence is also evident in the six octagonal fluted columns. The Italianate influence is reflected in the wooden tracery connecting the columns. The Gothic Revival influence can be seen in the balcony over the entrance.

No expense was spared for the interior of the house either. The entranceway is flanked by double parlors with marble mantels. Light from the chandeliers is reflected into in the pier mirrors located between the job

Errolton, a blending of Greek Revival, Italianate and Gothic Revival architecture, was built in 1848 for William B. Weaver.

Each of Errolton's double parlors has chandeliers that reflect into infinity in the gilded mirrors.

doors at each end of the parlors. One of the home's most stylish touches is the joined gold cornices over the mirrors. Running over the mirrors and the windows is a continuous gold-leaf cornice. The centers of the parlor ceilings are decorated with plaster medallions in the acanthus-leaf pattern.

Because of Errolton's elegance, Confederate president Jefferson Davis spent the night here in 1863. Davis, who had stopped by Columbus to attend a meeting of the Mississippi state legislature, had been visiting the Whitfield House in the daytime. He was awakened during the night by hundreds of citizens who had gathered under his bedroom window to serenade him. Delighted by the show of support, Davis donned a robe over his nightshirt and addressed the crowd.

Nellie Weaver, William B. Weaver's flamboyant daughter, was eight years old at the time. Davis's visit to Columbus was not the only historical event that was burned into her memory. In 1866, when Nellie was eleven years old, she observed a group of ladies from Columbus march to Friendship Cemetery and place flowers on the graves of soldiers. She recalled the reluctance with which they placed flowers on the graves of the Union soldiers as well. The ladies' noble gesture of respect was the foundation of what has become known as Memorial Day.

When Nellie was a teenager, she attended Columbus Female Institute, along with the other daughters of the town's most prominent families. She was known around town for her fashionable taste in clothing. Nellie was able to make a fashion statement even during Reconstruction, when she started a trend by sewing patches on her dresses. Because Nellie loved being the center of attention, she frequently appeared in amateur theatrical productions in Columbus. In 1875, Nellie created a local sensation with her performance as Lucy in Sheridan's *The Rival*. The play was held at the old Gilmore House. Even though some of the people in attendance suggested that Nellie pursue an acting career in New York City, she refused because the acting profession was not considered to be a proper occupation for a well-bred southern lady.

Nellie's thespian talents and the publicity that came with them led to invitations to dances throughout Columbus. Nellie was always the "Belle of the Ball" when she showed up at these exclusive social occasions. Naturally, Nellie attracted the attention of the town's most eligible young bachelors, who asked her to accompany them to dances, picnics and concerts and on boat rides.

Although she enjoyed the attention she received from all her local beaux, Nellie did not consider any of them to be suitable husband material. True romance finally entered her life in 1877 in the form of a handsome young man named Charles Tucker. He had just recently arrived in Columbus from Fredericksburg, Virginia, when a fire broke out at one of the local homes. Charles handed his coat to a bystander and assisted the firemen with extinguishing fire. Nellie, who was watching nearby, was impressed with Charles's total disregard for his own personal safety as he strode though the flames and smoke. A courtship soon followed, and the couple fell deeply in love. As was the custom of the day, Nellie etched her name on a pane of window glass in the south parlor of her home around the date of her marriage. Nellie and Charles were married at 8:30 p.m. on February 28, 1878.

Unfortunately, their story-book marriage was short-lived, and the couple parted just a few years later. Left with a daughter to raise, Ellen, Nellie was forced by necessity to become a tutor. She taught the children and grandchildren of her friends in one of the servants' quarters, which she converted into a classroom. Her primary focus in life was providing for herself and her little girl; the upkeep of the family home was secondary in importance. Consequently, the once proud home became increasingly dilapidated as the years passed. When Nellie became an old woman, her relatives pleaded with her to sell her house and move into an apartment, but she refused. She spent her later years sitting in her rocking chair on the front porch, entertaining anyone who would listen with stories from Columbus's "glory days." One day, when Nellie was in her eighties, she was walking through one of the double parlors when her dress caught fire in one of the fireplaces. Nellie died from her burns not long thereafter. The house was passed down to her heirs, Nell Wall and Walter Weaver Kennedy.

One of the locals who were regaled by Nellie's stores was Doug Bateman. "She knew everything that was going on," Bateman said, "all kinds of stories of skeletons in the very best closets." Around 1950, Bateman was approached by his friend Walter Weaver Kennedy, who was upset because Nell Wall was intent on selling her half of the house. The men talked for a while, and then Kennedy asked Bateman, "Why don't you buy the house?" Bateman discussed the offer with his mother, Mrs. Erroldine Bateman, who was an accomplished painter. She found the deal difficult to resist and purchased Wall's half of the house. Mrs. Bateman bought Kennedy's half after he moved to Florida. Once she took full possession of the house, she renamed it Errolton and began renovating it, with Doug's help.

The Batemans did not fully anticipate the toll that years of destructive tenants, vandalism and neglect had taken—peeling wallpaper and cheap partitions used to divide the main rooms into apartments. They also had to repair the holes in the rooms and replace the rotted floors. One day while Doug and his mother were supervising the workmen, Mrs. Bateman noticed the name "Nellie" etched into one of the few remaining windows that had not been broken. She realized the historical value of her discovery and was determined to preserve the window. Unfortunately, a careless workman leaned his ladder against the window and cracked it. Reluctantly, the Batemans disposed of the shards of glass and replaced the window.

Several weeks later, Doug's wife, Chebie, was passing through the back parlor when she noticed that the sun was shining on a recently reupholstered blue sofa. She walked over to the window to pull down the shade when she made a startling discovery: Nellie's name was back on the window in the same place it had been on the previous window. Surprisingly, neither Doug nor his wife was disturbed by the possibility that their house might be haunted. "Well," Doug thought, "we've got a ghost. That's great! There's no other explanation. It's becoming to the house. I had no fear. Miss Nellie liked me—she was a very friendly, lovable lady. There was no cause to fear her ghost. If it wasn't Miss Nellie who scratched her name on those window panes, we don't know how it happened."

Nellie's ghost has made only a few appearances inside the house over the years. "A time after we moved in, the front door would open and close—and nobody would be there," Bateman said. "I always got up and looked and never found anybody or anything. Then this door opening and closing stopped. I don't know why."

Anna Gaines, who has been serving as a guide in her parents' house during the Pilgrimage of Homes since she was a little girl, said that several times while growing up in the house, she heard disembodied footsteps on the stairs. For now, Nellie seems content to let her

An etching of Nellie Weaver's first name mysteriously reappeared after the original pane of glass was accidentally broken and replaced with a new pane of glass.

ghostly signature on the window serve as an indelible reminder of her years in the house and her lasting contributions to the lore of Columbus.

TEMPLE HEIGHTS

In 1836, General Richard T. Brownrigg came to Lowndes County from Edenton, North Carolina, where he had served in the state legislature. Even though he had studied medicine, Brownrigg never set up a practice. His overriding goal was to "strike it rich" in the fertile prairie of East Mississippi as a cotton planter. He began by purchasing a sizable tract of land from John Pitchlynn. Over the next few years, Brownrigg became one of the founders of the town of West Point. The ferry he set up between West Point and Columbus was instrumental in fostering the growth of both towns. In the

Richard T. Brownrigg built Temple Heights in 1837 for his wife and their five children.

ten years that Brownrigg lived in East Mississippi, he made a reputation for himself as a very civic-minded individual. Not only was he the senior warden for St. Paul's Episcopal Church, but he was also a member of the first board of trustees for the Mississippi Female College in 1838.

In 1839, Brownrigg began construction of an imposing house on top of a hill in Columbus. He modeled the home after his wife's family residence on the Albemarle Sound in South Carolina. Indeed, the floor plan of the house that was to become Temple Heights bears a close resemblance to that of homes on the Atlantic seaboard, with two rooms and a hallway on each of its four levels. The exterior of his house, with its two-story Doric columns and balcony, reflects the style that was so popular among the successful cotton planters in the mid-nineteenth century. Because the hall ran full length on the east side of the house, the chimneys were built on the west side. The interior of the house, designed in the Federal style, was equally impressive. Black marble mantels were installed on the main floor. The locks were made by the British firm of Carpenter and Company. The grain on the doors was painted—a common practice in those days. The millwork was made in the corner-block design.

Unfortunately, Brownrigg spent only a few years in the house he had spent so much time designing and furnishing. In December 1846, he disappeared and was assumed drowned in the 1846–47 flood that devastated the town of West Point. In 1847, Thomas W. Harris, a politician from Georgia, bought the house at public auction for $3,350. Like Brownrigg, Harris was a wealthy planter. He was also a probate judge for Lowndes County. Once he took possession of the house, Harris set about changing its exterior appearance to resemble that of an ancient Greek temple. He created a magnificent entranceway on the east side by adding ten Doric columns and two galleries, turning the house into a classic example of Greek Revival architecture.

Several different families have owned and lived in Temple Heights. Following Harris's death, his son sold the house to his wife's sister, Mrs. Francis Jane Butler Fontaine. She is remembered as one of the ladies who placed flowers from their gardens on the graves of fallen Confederate and Union soldiers in Friendship Cemetery and began the tradition that is now known as Memorial Day. In 1887, the J.H. Kennebrew family bought the house from Mrs. Fontaine for $2,600. The house remained in the Kennebrew family for the next seventy-eight years. Because Mrs. Kennebrew wanted to make sure her daughters would always have a place to live, her will reads that Temple Heights could not be sold until all of them were married. Two of the daughters never married and retained possession of Temple Heights until 1965, when local businessman Kirk Eggar bought the house with the intention of selling it to someone who would preserve it.

In 1968, Eggar sold the house to Dixie and Carl Butler, a couple of educators who had been recommended to him by their friends Bill Lee Sanders, Virginia Hooper and Ed Keaton. "I came here in 1965 to coach swimming," Carl said. "I'd always been interested in historic properties and knew about Temple Heights but was told it was uninhabitable. It was in terrible shape, visually; it had not been painted in forty years." Impressed by their commitment to restore the old home to its former glory, Eggar allowed the Butlers to pay $1,000 down; the rest would be paid after they finished graduate school at Peabody and Vanderbilt in Nashville. Carl and Dixie were married in 1968 and moved into Temple Heights the next year.

Restoring the old mansion was not an overnight affair. The couple began by cleaning and painting one room at a time. Carl and Dixie spent years transforming Temple Heights into the architectural gem that it had been throughout most of the nineteenth century. "Renovating this house has been a good hobby for us," Dixie said. "People say, 'You must have a lot of money to fix up the house like this,' but my husband and I are both schoolteachers.

We've learned to shop carefully. We learned that you have to find the right thing in the wrong place. Some of the furniture was given to me by my grandmother." Today, Temple Heights stands as one of Mississippi's best examples of period restoration. It is also one of the most haunted houses in the entire state.

Carl and Dixie realized that something otherworldly might be inhabiting their house not long after they moved in. The tranquility of their sanctuary from the noise and bustle of the modern world was disrupted by unexplained sounds. Several times, the Butlers heard the sound of pottery and glassware breaking. When they ran into the next room, they were shocked to find that nothing was out of place. "The most memorable crashing sound was in the summer of 1969," Dixie said.

> We had the Olympic swimmer Don Showlander here. My husband coached a local swim team. We had had a brunch. When we got breakfast, they had gone out to do something with some of the "swimming" children. They were coming back for lunch. Don's wife, Penny, stayed here. A friend of mine also remained behind to clean up from one meal before the next one. The three of us were sitting downstairs on a sofa, and we heard a loud crash up here. All three of us jumped up and ran all over the house, but we couldn't find a window that had closed or a picture that had fallen off the wall. We couldn't find anything on the porch either. To this day, I have no idea what it was. I wasn't scared when it happened, but this was the first summer when we were here, and it might have been one of the first times we heard something weird in the house.

Carl and Dixie eventually reached the point where they became accustomed to hearing unexplained noises. However, not everyone took the noises in stride. In 1997, a visiting professor from the Mississippi University for Women, Bridget Pieschel, was attending a supper club at Temple Heights. Eight people were present—Carl, Dixie, Mr. and Mrs. Davis, Mr. and Mrs. Richardson and Bridget and her husband, Steve. At 9:00 p.m., just before dessert, Bridget left the dining room table to go up to the second floor to the only bathroom in the house. "You leave the dining room and the parlor area, and you walk up a fairly steep flight of stairs to a landing," Bridget said. "Then you turn, and you walk up a few more stairs. The bathroom is right there, on the landing." At the time, the seven other people inside the house were seated around the dining table. She entered the bathroom, and a couple minutes later, she heard someone coming up the stairs. "Those stairs have a very distinctive creak," Bridget said.

> *You can't step on them without making a noise. Then I heard somebody walk to the outside of the bathroom door. So I thought, "OK, I'd better hurry up. Somebody wants to use the bathroom." I finished and washed my hands. When I opened the door, nobody was standing there. I thought somebody was in the other bedroom, so I said, "I'm finished. You can come in now." Nobody was on the second floor. I didn't know what had happened. I thought it was strange, but it still hadn't occurred to me that it wasn't somebody from the dining room coming up to go to the bathroom.*

Bridget returned to the dining room to find everyone seated at the table eating dessert. She told them she had left the bathroom and that it was empty now, but they gave her a quizzical look. Bridget said, "Somebody was obviously trying to get into the bathroom while I was there. I'm out. You can go on up." Once again, the dinner guests stared at her in stunned silence. Then Dixie said, "Nobody left the table to go up to the bathroom. We're not the kind of people to play practical jokes on each other." Trying to laugh away her discomfort, Bridget insisted she had heard somebody come up the stairs, walk down the hall and stand outside the door. Dixie waited a few seconds before saying, "Well, it must have been Elizabeth trying to get into the bathroom."

Elizabeth was the most eccentric of Reverend Kennebrew's two unmarried daughters. As a young woman, Elizabeth rejected all of her suitors. She lived out the remainder of her life as what people referred to as an "old maid." The eccentric behavior she had exhibited as a girl became even more obvious in her later years. Older residents of Columbus spoke of seeing her walk around town wearing mercurochrome for rouge and lipstick and chalk dust for face powder. She completed her bizarre look by dyeing her hair red. Her behavior was equally strange. Elizabeth is said to have worn heavy winter clothes in the summertime. She explained that she was getting ready to travel to Alaska or St. Petersburg.

Elizabeth's ghost was quite possibly sighted by the Butlers' landlady, Mrs. Wakefield, during their first year in the house. Mrs. Wakefield usually stayed in the second-floor guest room. One day, she was leaving her room when she saw what she described as a "wispy thing" float from the third-floor steps to the second-floor landing. She was so alarmed by her encounter that she ran inside the room and placed a chair against the door. Upon reflection afterward, Mrs. Wakefield realized that if what she saw really was a ghost, placing a chair against the door would not have helped at all.

Elizabeth may have appeared to a friend of Dixie's as well. In 1991, at the end of one of the Butlers' dinner parties, the topic of conversation turned to ghosts, and one of the guests made a surprising revelation. She said that several months earlier, she had been guiding tourists through the house. While taking a break between tours, she was walking down the hallway when she saw a strange woman standing in the center of the Butlers' bedroom. Visibly shaken, she rushed downstairs but told no one what she had seen. A few days later, she was talking to an elderly acquaintance of hers, and she described the spectral figure. The lady listened intently and replied, "The lady you are describing sounds just like Elizabeth Kennebrew."

Elizabeth is not the only female spirit haunting Temple Heights. One night, while Carl's parents were visiting, Dixie decided to go to bed. While she was lying in bed, she heard her in-laws talking about the guest room's previous tenants. Carl said, "We know somebody named 'Laura' was here because her name is written in pencil on the door." This particular Laura is probably Laura Kennebrew, one of the Kennebrew sisters. When Carl and his parents walked up stairs, his mother said, "Well, show me." Carl looked at the door, but he couldn't find the name anywhere. Carl walked into the bedroom where Dixie was reading and said, "Dixie, come show my parents where Laura wrote her name." Dixie climbed out of bed and looked at the door, but she couldn't find the name either. Frustrated, Dixie grabbed her flashlight and examined every door on the first and second floors, but the name was gone.

Apparently, Laura's ghost has reclaimed the guest room. "I had a friend named Theo Patterson." Dixie said. "She lives in Jackson and was the curator of an old mansion for many years. She spent the night in the guest room. The next morning, she said she felt a cold presence in the room. She didn't see it; she felt it." Interestingly enough, Dixie never sensed the entity when she was in the room.

Theo Patterson was not the only one who seems to have attracted the spirits inside the house. "One of our cats was sitting on a sofa," Dixie said. "One of our friends took a photograph, and there was a glowing ball of mist." Dixie believed that the photograph was proof that her house was haunted. "Sometimes, the cat will be looking at something, and you will wonder what he's looking at."

Temple Heights's haunted reputation grew, at least in part, due to the large number of people who have toured the historic house. In 1994, Nancy Wheeley, a librarian at Mississippi University for Women, was asked to lead a group of conventioneers through Dixie's house. "I arrived wearing my hoopskirt," Nancy said.

> *While the group was touring, Dixie had another group of tourists in the home, so I sat on the steps of the third floor. The stairways are all on one side of the house. The stairs leading to the basement were below where I was sitting. Suddenly, I heard music coming from somewhere in the house. Dixie asked me if I heard music. I told her that I did, and she said, "I don't have anything turned on." I said, "Elizabeth?" and she said, "Yes."*

Dixie told Nancy that Elizabeth is the ghost that plays the Victrola on the fourth floor of the house. However, Dixie never heard the spectral music herself.

Dixie had her own brush with the paranormal back in the 1970s. She walked into the entrance hall one day when she saw the figure of a woman standing in the corner. After the specter vanished, Dixie was aware that she had made the acquaintance with another of Temple Heights's residents. She suspects that the apparition she saw might have been the spirit of Annie Fountaine, whose name is etched into the window pane next to the entrance door. The pane is cracked, but the name is still visible, possibly because it was scratched into the surface of the glass with a diamond ring.

One of Dixie's last ghostly experiences inside the house took place in October 2008. One of the fall decorations that were placed around the house was a small scarecrow. One morning, she set the scarecrow on the nightstand with its head facing inside the bedroom. When she returned to the bedroom later in the afternoon, the scarecrow's head had been turned in the opposite direction. She asked the housekeeper if she had moved the scarecrow, but the woman said she had not touched it at all. That night, Dixie decided to turn the scarecrow once again so that it was facing inside. The next morning, she woke up to find that the scarecrow was facing outside once again.

This writer interviewed Dixie Butler one last time in March 2015 during the Pilgrimage of Homes. I asked her if anything unusual had occurred recently. She said that the spirits in the house seem to have quieted down, although she did occasionally hear some sounds at night that she could not identify. At the time of this writing, Temple Heights was for sale. One can only hope that the new tenants share the Butlers' love for Temple Heights and their acceptance of the spirits that refuse to leave.

THE BARKER-BUNCH HOUSE

An article by staff reporter Martha Neyman about the haunting of the Barker-Bunch House on Seventh Street appeared in the April 12, 1998 edition of the *Commercial Dispatch*. The house was built in 1839. Jamie and Elizabeth Lott moved into the historic home during the summer of 1997. The paranormal activity started up while the family of five was unpacking. Mrs. Lott was working inside one of the rooms when she decided to move furniture in another part of the house. When she returned to the room, she was surprised to find that the books she'd stacked up inside a wardrobe before she left were now scattered all over the floor.

Elizabeth Lott was not the only family member who sensed from the outset that something unearthly was inside the old house. Her adolescent son was playing with his remote-controlled car one evening in the downstairs kitchen. After a while, the boy became tired and went to his bedroom, unaware that he still had the remote control in his hand. Shortly after midnight, his parents were awakened by a humming sound coming from the kitchen. To their amazement, the car was moving on its own, back and forth, across the kitchen. They tried to turn the little car off manually, but to no avail. The only way they could stop the car was by removing the batteries.

Not long thereafter, Mr. and Mrs. Lott were lying in bed asleep. Suddenly, at 2:00 a.m., they felt a strong breeze blow diagonally across their bed. The accompanying sound was that of a car barreling down a highway at a high rate of speed with the radio blasting. They checked to see if their bedroom window was cracked open slightly, but it was shut tight.

The paranormal activity continued over the next few months. Mrs. Lott was perusing the aisles of a gift shop when she spotted a figurine that resembled her youngest child. She continued her shopping and found figurines of a brother and sister that reminded her of her oldest children. When she returned home with her finds, Mrs. Lott placed them on a table in the foyer. The figurines were facing one another at a slight angle. When she woke up the next morning and walked into the foyer, she discovered that the figurines were facing in a completely different direction with their backs to one another. Thinking that one of her children had been playing with them, she rearranged the figurines back to their original position. She did not think about them again until the next morning, when she found them looking away from one another once again. She talked to the children, but they said they hadn't touched the figurines. The unseen hand continued to move the figurines around until Mrs. Lott finally gave up and left them the way the entity wanted them.

The disturbances in the Lott household seem to be the work of a poltergeist, which Theresa Cheung, author of *The Element Encyclopedia of Ghosts & Hauntings*, defines as "a ghost or energy which specializes in making sounds or moving things about a house or building, often resulting in breakages." Although poltergeists have been known to be destructive and, in some cases, even malevolent, for the most part, they are mischievous nuisances. Most poltergeist activity occurs when an adolescent girl is living in the house. The Lott family would probably agree that the poltergeist that inhabited their home was probably more intent on disrupting their routine than on inflicting actual harm.

LOWNDES COUNTY

JOE EUBANKS PLANTATION

According to the 1860 census, 436,631 slaves were living in Mississippi, outnumbering the 352,901 white persons living there. The census also indicates that slave owners in Mississippi numbered 30,043—or 8.7 percent of the total white population. The 1860 census shows that in Lowndes County, 16,370 slaves were owned by 120 slaveholders who held 40 or more slaves. That figure accounts for 8,960 slaves, or 53 percent of the county's total. The remainder of the slaves in Lowndes County were held by a total of 876 slaveholders.

The lives of many ex-slaves from Mississippi were recorded by field workers for the Federal Writers Project between 1937 and 1938. Field workers were given a list of twenty categories of sample questions covering the subjects' experiences as slaves, their memories of the Civil War and their lives after the Civil War. Because the interviewers had no tape recorders, they recorded their interviews with pencil and paper. Some interviewers attempted to reproduce the dialects of the ex-slaves, while others simply rewrote the slaves' narratives in Standard English. Most interviewers rarely strayed from their prepared list of questions.

One of the ex-slaves from Lowndes County who was interviewed in 1937 was Jerry Eubanks. He was born in Atlanta about 1846 to Alice and Jerry Hamilton. He had six brothers and sisters, but at the time of the interview, he could remember only one of them, Warren. When Jerry was twelve years old, a speculator named Jack Hart sold him to Dr. Sam Hamilton of Rome, Georgia. Financial difficulties forced Hamilton to sell Jerry to Joe Eubanks for $1,100. Eubanks owned a plantation ten miles north of Columbus. "I was Ole Miss's regular carriage driver," Jerry said. "I weared special drivers' clothes. I weared one of dese high beaver hats and sot on de outside of de carriage." Jerry also worked in the "big house" as a dining room servant. "Dey had so much, dat even what was left in de plate was nuff to feed me," Jerry said.

Jerry went on to say that Joe Eubanks had two house servants and eighteen slaves who worked the land. "Not on Joe Eubanks' place was any nigger whipped, 'cause he was our boss," Jerry said. "Our folks fared well to what some did." Joe Eubanks and his wife, Melia, had six children: three boys and three girls. "Miss Melia died at Waverly," Jerry said. "I think she was a little connected to de Colonel Young."

One of the interviewer's prepared questions concerned the folkways of the ex-slaves. Jerry Eubanks was asked about his beliefs regarding ghosts. "Well, no, I ain't seed no ghosts," Jerry said,

> *but I come so near, I thought I see'd 'em. Here's a story what's true. It used to be so we had to watch the gin to keep people from stealing cotton, and we was watching about a hundred. I was dar. Dem ghosts was dar too, and dey run us home. Dey was little bitty low things. . . . You know dis was in de Delta at Silver City. Some niggers had drowned in de river. A whole lot of 'em had fell out of dis gin house, and dey come back. About eleven o'clock, de whistle blowed jes like fire, and dar wasn't a bit of fire, but we run, and de agent went hisself next night, and he was run off too.*
>
> *Den I know anoder time where a ghost come to Mr. Cox's over de oder side of Waverly. He was settin' readin' his paper, and his light went out. Somein said "Phew!" He lighted it four times. Mr. Charlie Cox said something said "Phew!" every time. Mr. Cox left dat house and went to his sister.*
>
> *We went to a dance out at Dr. Brothers' brother's home. We was upstairs and fo' God we was a sittin' there, preachers, too, and a door was pitched down on us. Oh, I done some running! Dat house is dere now. . . . Looks like de house goin' be tore down every night. Dey jes runs around all over de house.*

Jerry Eubanks ended his ghost stories by commenting on the large number of ghosts in Lowndes County: "Dere is lots of evil around Columbus. Dey puts horse shoes over de door, but dat don't turne de evil spirits."

Prairie

The Gulf Ordnance Munitions Plant

During World War II, millions of Americans contributed to the war effort, not only on the battlefields, but on the homefront as well. In fact, the war could not have been won without the weapons produced in American factories and ammunition plants. The Gulf Ordnance Munitions Plant in Prairie, Mississippi, was one of the largest ammunition plants in the entire country. Construction of the plant was contracted to Procter & Gamble, which had built a shell-loading plant in Milan, Tennessee. Thanks to the support of Senators Wall Doxey and Theodore Bilbo, Monroe County in Mississippi was chosen as the site of the plant. Prairie's flat land and its isolation made the little town a prime location. The federal government gave the landowners thirty days to relocate. Between 150 and 200 private homes were razed to make room for the plant. The Ferguson-Oman Company was selected as the primary contractor for the project. The groundbreaking ceremony was held in April 1942. Approximately ten thousand people worked twenty-four/seven to construct the plant on 6,720 acres of land. To prevent explosions from spreading throughout the entire complex, the contractors fortified the walls of the structures so that explosions would be directed upward through the roofs, which were loosely attached to the buildings. To reduce the likelihood of explosions occurring, the contractors used only explosive-proof parts in water fountains and telephones. Only florescent lighting was installed in the shell-loading buildings. Auxiliary buildings constructed by

Groups of paranormal investigators have taken some eerie photographs and EVPs at the Gulf Ordnance Plant. *Photo courtesy of Jeremy Griffin.*

the Ferguson-Oman Company included staff houses, a cafeteria, lighting power houses, staff houses, dormitories, guard houses, a firefighting system and loading and administrative buildings. In addition to the 125 buildings, the Gulf Ordnance Plant included twenty miles of gravel roads and twenty-seven miles of railroad track.

Line 1 of the Gulf Ordnance Plant started operations in November 1942. After the Gulf Ordnance Plant commenced operations, it became the second-largest business in Mississippi. Between six and seven thousand people, many of whom were women, worked in the plant, producing one-hundred-pound bombs; rocket launchers; naval tracer ammunition; and twenty-, fifty-, fifty-seven- and sixty-seven-millimeter shells. Many of the workers came from Corinth and Macon, Mississippi, and from several small towns in west Alabama. They were transported to the plant on a bus known as the "Mississippian" and on a small train called "The Doodlebug." Supplies were delivered by trains and trucks and were stored in twenty-five warehouses. Between four and six workers rode in each train car. Newspaper reporters were not allowed inside the plant. However, the plant had its own newspaper called *The Tracer*. Nearby Aberdeen thrived during the war. So many workers went to town on their off-hours that the cafés were open all day and night. Approximately 25 percent of the ammunition used by the U.S. military was produced at the Gulf Ordnance Munitions Plant.

Warheads were made in the three-story building, which is still standing. TNT was brought to the rear of the building in carts. The TNT was melted in four "cookers." It was then piped down to the first floor and put into the warheads of one-hundred-pound bombs.

The plant closed down after 1945, not long after the dropping of the atomic bombs on Japan, primarily because of the diminished need for munitions. Most of the buildings were razed by the U.S. military. The people who worked there acquired skills that helped them find work in the private sector. Part of the property is occupied by a cattle ranch operated by Mississippi State University. Only a few crumbling ruins, bunkers, tunnels and a half-million-gallon water tank remain, faint remnants of the lives that once called this place home. The Gulf Ordnance Munitions Plant may be nothing more than a few dilapidated buildings surrounded by bushes and covered in vines, but it is still home to a variety of ghosts.

Because factories were dangerous places to work at in the 1940s, one assumes that the spirits of the people who died while on the job are haunting the old plant. However, only two people died there between 1942 and 1945. One man hit a train on his way to work. Another was "sprayed" while standing too close to the cookers and severely burned. He died not long thereafter.

According to the Amory-based Mystic Mississippi Paranormal Society, most of the spirits people have encountered on the site are the ghosts of Civil War soldiers who died in the Battle of Okolona. On February 11, 1864, Union general William Smith made his way through northeast Mississippi, ravaging the countryside, while General William Tecumseh Sherman led his troops to Meridian. On February 20, Sherman left Meridian, and Smith headed for Okolona. On February 22, General Nathan Bedford Forrest attacked Smith's army at Okolona. Following the death of his younger brother, General Jeffrey Forest, Nathan Bedford Forrest led another assault on Smith's army to exact vengeance. The Union army withdrew and initiated an eleven-mile running battle. Eventually, General Smith was forced to retreat to the Tennessee border. Not only did a number of soldiers die in the area now occupied by the Gulf Ordnance Plant, but some of them were buried there as well, just behind the railroad line.

Linda Callahan and her sister, Sammie, worked security shifts at the Gulf Ordnance Munitions Plant back when it was a facility for Walker Manufacturing. Linda said that one Saturday night, she received a frantic phone call on her answering machine from her sister, who was working all alone at the old plant. "Linda, if you're there, please pick up the phone! Please, oh God, help me!" In Sammie's harrowing message, she described the spectral figures of a nurse and a wounded soldier that suddenly materialized in front of her. Sammie described, in great detail, the nurse's white uniform with cuffs and the soldier's gray coat with brass buttons. She distinctly recalled that the soldier was wearing black shoes and had a bloodied bandage on his head. Linda believed everything her sister told her because she had also witnessed paranormal activity inside the plant. "Take my word for it," Linda said. "I don't know what it is, and I don't want to find out for myself, but I believe it with all my heart."

The Mystic Mississippi Paranormal Society, which has raised money for local organizations through its ghost tours of the plant, has had some compelling personal experiences. In an old munitions tunnel, a dominant spirit named Phillip made his presence known to the group. People on the tours have captured orbs, heard strange sounds and experienced drops in temperature. So much ghostly activity has been reported from the site that an episode of the television series *My Ghost Story* was filmed here.

Two investigations by the Mystic Mississippi Paranormal Society were particularly memorable. On October 3, 2009, inside the Main Ordnance Building, the group captured an orb and the image of a torso with no head or legs on the first floor. After a while, the members noticed that the batteries in their equipment were drained. Several people felt as if they were being watched the entire time. During one of the group's ghost-hunting experiences in 2010, it recorded the voice of a spirit that identified himself as Dale. The group also recorded two other startling EVPs: a moan and a voice that said, "Just leave." Orbs were photographed inside and outside of the building. The most frightening visual evidence of the evening was the picture of a face looking around the corner of a wall.

Another investigation of the Gulf Ordnance Plant took place during a podcast called *Kill Pop Culture Halloween Special 2015*. During the night of October 30, 2015, the investigators conducted a Spirit Box session. When one of the investigators said, "Rob" (the name of one of the other investigators), the Sprit Box responded with "Robbie." The investigators also heard a male voice say, "Get out!" and a female voice say, "Clearly." Later on, they visited the three-story building and several tunnels, most of which are flooded. One of the tunnels the investigators were able to walk through was the "Suicide Tunnel," so named because a number of young people are said to have killed themselves there. Supposedly, people have scrawled messages on the walls of the tunnel, pleading with despondent people to seek help instead of ending it all.

The investigators all collected a startling photograph image on October 30. Rob was walking around one of the tunnels taking random photographs. "Germ (another investigator) was behind me," Rob said. "On one of the photographs was a well-arranged formation of what I thought were dust particles. At first, I thought I had taken a picture of Germ, but the figure was too tall. It looked like a pumpkin head with wide hips. I posted the photograph on our Facebook page."

Another legend associated with the Gulf Ordnance Plant is strange "booming" sounds people reporting hearing in the general area. Rob said that he heard the explosions when he was in grade school in Prairie. He went on to say that one of the explosions was so loud that one of the girls was knocked out of her chair. Rumors spread that old warheads were being disposed of at the old plant. The official explanation, though, was that the explosions came from a mining operation in the area.

Anyone wishing to visit the Gulf Ordnance Munitions Plant should receive permission from the landowners before venturing onto the property. Take Highway 45 ALT North toward West Point and Tupelo. Continue twenty miles on Highway 45 ALT North through West Point. Turn right on Prairie Road/Highway 387. Follow the green highway sign pointing to Prairie. Stay on Prairie Road/Highway 387 for two miles. Continue past a white water tower. Turn left down a dirt road to a dead end. You should be able to see the remains of the buildings from there.

STARKVILLE

GEORGE HALL

The Agricultural and Mechanical College of Mississippi, one of the land grant colleges created by the 1862 Morrill Act, was established by the Mississippi state legislature on February 28, 1878. The first students were admitted in the fall of 1880. The first president of the college was Stephen D. Lee, a former general in the Confederate army. The Hatch Act was passed by Congress to set up the Agricultural Experiment Station in 1888. The 1914 Smith-Lever Act established extension offices in every county. The mission of the Agricultural and Mechanical College of Mississippi was extended once more by the 1917 Smith-Hughes Act, which provided funding for the training of teachers in vocational schools. The college was accredited by the Southern Association of Colleges and schools in 1926. The name of the college was changed to Mississippi State College in 1932. At this time, the institution included a number of separate colleges, including the College of Engineering (1902), the School of Industrial Pedagogy (1911), the Mississippi Agricultural Extension Service (1915) and the Division of Continuing Education (1919). In 1958, the name of the institution was changed once again, this time to Mississippi State University (MSU). The university's three-pronged mission now embraced learning, research and service. The Mississippi Agricultural and Forestry Experiment Station and the Mississippi State University Extension Service raised the public's awareness of the university. By the twenty-first century, the university's

Between 1878 and 1932, when the university was Mississippi A&M, students marched and practiced in the Drill Field in the center of campus. *Courtesy of Patrick Threatt.*

agricultural imperative was only part of the university's program offerings, which now include the College of Arts and Sciences, the Bagley College of Engineering, the College of Business and the College of Agriculture. Even though MSU is, in many ways, a progressive university, its past is prominently displayed in its historic buildings, two of which are reputed to be haunted.

Built in 1902, George Hall was named after James Z. George, a United States senator known as "the Great Commoner." He spearheaded the construction of the hospital that bears his name, George Memorial Hospital, which was considered one of the finest facilities of its day. Located next to MacGruder Hall and across from Lee Hall, the Colonial Revival building now houses University Relations. In the early 1900s, George Hall served as the school's infirmary during the deadliest epidemic in modern history. The influenza pandemic of 1918–19 infected 500 million people worldwide and took an estimated 20 to 50 million lives. A number of Mississippi State students succumbed to the virus as well. During this tragic time, the infected students were treated on the second floor; the basement of George Hall was converted into a temporary morgue, where the deceased students were embalmed. John Summerlot, resident director of Suttle Hall, said there are rumors that the ghosts of

George Hall, which served as the school infirmary during the influenza epidemic of 1918, may be haunted by the ghosts of infected students who died there. *Courtesy Patrick Threatt.*

these unfortunate students still wander around the floors of the building where they died. Although no witnesses of paranormal activity inside the building have come forward, Summerlot is not convinced there is nothing to these stories. "It [George Hall] was kind of creepy back then, and it is still creepy now."

Montgomery Hall

Montgomery Hall, built in the Beaux-Arts style, was named for W.B. Montgomery, a member of the board of trustees. In the early years, the building was known as the Scientific Building. The name was eventually changed to Montgomery Agricultural Hall. In recent years, Montgomery Hall was designated a Mississippi Landmark and a National Historical Place. Displaced Student Services, Educational Psychology and Counselor Education are now housed in the old building.

Rumors about the haunted activity inside Montgomery Hall can be traced back to an incident that occurred in the 1960s. Betty Self, an employee at

In the 1960s, a group of students performed occult rituals at Montgomery Hall.

the Mitchell Memorial Library, said that a group of students performed occult rituals inside the fourth floor of the building. They conducted séances and attempted to communicate with otherworldly spirits by means of Ouija boards. After the group's secret ceremonies were exposed, the members abandoned their meeting place, but they left behind tangible evidence of their dark rites. The dean of education, Roy Roby, claimed to have seen one of the group's satanic symbols: "I had been up there. They had a symbol with a six-pointed star with a dead bird in the center of the star." Robert Wolverton, a professor of foreign languages, saw the same symbols on the top floor. "We saw that some sort of cult had been there," Wolverton said. Because the top floor of Montgomery Hall is no longer in use, it may be difficult to determine whether any of the entities conjured up by the cult are still present.

WEST POINT

WAVERLY

Colonel George Hampton Young came to Mississippi from Oglethorpe County, Georgia. Young had studied law at Georgia's Franklin College and at Columbia College in New York. Afterward, he practiced law in Georgia and served in the state legislature. On March 31, 1836, the Choctaw Indians sold fifty thousand acres of farm- and timberland on the Tombigbee River to Colonel Young for $3,000. He selected as the site for his future home a gently sloping knoll a quarter of a mile from the river. However, it took twenty-two years before the construction of the home was completed. The British Isles were prominently represented in the house. Colonel Young named his home Waverly, after the series of novels written by his favorite author, Sir Walter Scott. The house was designed by an English architect named Pond. The Young family lived in a log cabin on the property while the house was being built. A Scotsman created the mantels and marble work. Two Irishmen did the ornate plasterwork. Young grew three thousand acres of cotton with the help of one thousand slaves.

As the result of Young's diligence and ingenuity, Waverly eventually became self-sustaining. At one time, Waverly had gardens, orchards, livestock, a cotton gin, a brick kiln, an icehouse and a brick-and-marble swimming pool complete with bathhouse. The Youngs also had their own leather tannery and lumber mill. In the plantation's heyday, they were able to produce everything from felt hats to saddle blankets and saddles. Colonel

Waverly was built in 1852 for George Hampton Young, who moved to West Point, Mississippi, from Georgia.

Young even burned pine knots to create gas, which was piped into fixtures in the main house and used for lighting.

Colonel Young's family thrived in their magnificent surroundings. Mrs. Young brought several boxwood plants from her former home as reminders of the family's ties with Georgia. Unfortunately, she died in the log cabin where she bore her children before the mansion was completed. Her six sons and four daughters grew up in Waverly. Four of the children took their vows in the parlor under an arched alcove known as the "wedding alcove." The library was the colonel's favorite room, where he read his favorite books, conducted his business affairs and entertained his friends. The National Fox Hunters' Association was founded in the library in 1893. The lavish parties held at the mansion lasted days and even weeks. The Youngs entertained their guests with foxhunts, barbecues and swim parties.

All of Colonel Young's sons served as Confederate officers during the Civil War. One of his sons, Beverley, died in a New York hospital in 1863 from wounds he had received at Gettysburg. Many of the guests who frequented parties at Waverly during the war years were officers.

General Nathan Bedford Forrest is said to have visited Waverly on several occasions.

The Young family retained possession of Waverly until 1913, when Colonel Young's last surviving son, Captain William Young, died. For the next fifty years, Waverly stood abandoned, frequented only by souvenir hunters, young people looking for an isolated spot for their parties and fraternity initiations and an assortment of "critters," including bats, squirrels, birds, opossums and insects. In 1962, Mr. and Mrs. Robert Allen Snow Jr., the owners of an antique shop in Philadelphia, Mississippi, bought Waverly and twenty acres of the original estate. By the time the Snows arrived at the old plantation, Waverly's grandeur had faded. Mrs. Young's once beautiful boxwoods had become fodder for deer and cattle. The exterior of the house was strangled with vines and brush. The doors were off their hinges. The shutters had been thrown in the brush. Approximately one hundred of the home's windows were broken, including two sections of the red Venetian glass at the main entrance. The massive marble slab steps were scattered over the grounds. Vandals had smashed the marble fireplaces. Cracks, spider webs and graffiti covered the walls. Protococcus had spread over the interior walls, and vines had grown through the broken windows. Mold was everywhere. Evidence that the birds had taken advantage of the broken windows was readily apparent. Chimney swifts roosted in the chimneys, sparrows made nests in the chandeliers and woodpeckers made holes in the walls and furniture. The cut-glass chandelier globes were gone. Someone had wrenched several gaslight sconces from the walls. Miraculously, three gold-leaf mirrors were still hanging in their original places on the first floor. The ornate plasterwork and millwork was in fairly good condition as well. Only 3 of the 718 mahogany spindles in the double stairs were gone.

The restoration process began when the family moved in on May 31, 1962. "All delays encountered during this work were expected," Donna said in 1986. "We expected to work on the house a lifetime, and after twenty years, we are painting again and still repairing." At times, the Snows and their four children lived in the same room during the restoration process. Over the next two decades, the Snows added a new roof and new porches. The old capitals on the columns were replaced with new ones. The Snows removed one of the columns; the replacement was re-grooved on sawhorses in the backyard. Painters worked steadily throughout the restoration process. Workers re-trimmed the octagonal cupola, which towers sixty-five feet over the entrance. The cupola's sixteen windows supplied the house with the nineteenth-century equivalent of air conditioning. After the cupola was

When this photograph was taken in 1936, Waverly had been abandoned for over twenty years. *Courtesy of the Library of Congress.*

Waverly's now beautiful grounds were overgrown with strangling vegetation when the Snows took possession of the property in 1962.

restored, an exact replica of Colonel Young's copper-covered finial was placed on the dome. No important structural alterations were made to the original building. The kitchen had been attached to the house since 1887. The indoor bathrooms were installed in the existing closets.

One of the most dangerous parts of the renovation was the removal of some of the old house's non-human occupants while they were restoring the plaster in the hallway in the dome area. After the Snows removed some of old plaster and lathing, they discovered thousands of bees and a large number of bee cones. With the assistance of Artley Jack and Price Sykes, the Snows attempted to remove the bees with a vacuum cleaner. Even though the men covered every exposed part of their bodies, they all suffered multiple stings during the "eviction." Even a photographer for the *Commercial Dispatch*, Joe Sarcone, was stung on top of his head. Once most of the bees had been removed, the men began cutting out the cones. While the bees were swarming around the workers, Robert Snow sprinkled them with water to impair their flying ability. When they were finished, the men were delighted to find that they had removed over 150 pounds of honey from the wall. The Snows divided the honey among the workers and their friends. Despite their efforts to repel the bees with insecticide, the Snows were unsuccessful in their efforts to get rid of the bees on the porch because they enter the capitals through the openings in the Ionic scrolls.

Thanks to the Snows' years of hard work and research, Waverly has become, once again, one of the most magnificent nineteenth-century showplaces of the Deep South. The grand entranceway opens up into an octagonal hall thirty-eight feet in diameter. The two winding staircases on each side of the house converge on the upper floors. From an architectural viewpoint, the stairwell is one of the most distinctive features of the mansion, with its third- and fourth-floor balconies overlooking the main floor. The second floor contains bedrooms twenty-two by twenty-five feet. All of the rooms have three or four windows that can be opened up for cross ventilation. All of the stair railings are made of walnut. Two stairs lead from the balcony hall to a half story designed as trunk rooms. The observatory rises sixty-five feet from the main floor. Suspended from the observatory ceiling is a magnificent chandelier illuminating the bedrooms and the floors below. It hangs in the exact center of a lovely molded plaster medallion. Two tall wall mirrors stand in the foyer. The mirror on the west wall is cracked, the unfortunate result of setting a lamp too close to it at a dance during the Civil War. The gold leaf in the parlor mirror was reworked in Mobile. None of the four antique mirrors in Waverly needed re-silvering.

This beautiful chandelier illuminates the bedrooms and lower floors.
Sparrows were living in nests in the chandelier when the Snows moved in.
Courtesy Library of Congress.

The furnishings inside the house reflected the opulent lifestyle of the original occupants. The clock in the library is set in ivory. The andirons in the library fireplace are French iron and brass. The walnut gun rack in the library is original to the house. The built-in secretary was used as the post office for the plantation. Inside the master bedroom is a large half-tester bed. The chandelier in the middle of the bedroom is brass with globes of Waterford crystal. The centerpiece of the dining room is the mahogany table with Chippendale chairs. The butler's desk is highlighted with Paris and Venetian glass. The dining room chandelier is French gilt with ribbed globes. Three pieces of rare Belter furniture—two chairs and a settee—are located in a first-floor bedroom.

Waverly has won a number of important awards over the years. In 1968, it received the "Restoration of the Year" award from the American Association for State and Local History. The award was presented to Donna and Robert Snow by Dr. W.R. Mortensen, president of the association, who said that Waverly was chosen for the honor over thousands of entries from the United States and Canada. He praised the Snows for their "master craftsmanship, their impeccable taste [and] their appreciation of beauty." Then, in 1973, a National Historic Landmark plaque was presented to Waverly before a large group of invited guests, governmental dignitaries and tourists.

As a result of the positive publicity the Snows received locally for their restoration efforts, Waverly soon attracted the attention of the national media. In 1965, the *Commercial Appeal* from Memphis did a story on Robert Snow's collection of exotic birds, including oriental pheasants, Japanese silky chickens, gold-billed ducks and India blue peafowl. In 1984, a crew from *House and Garden* magazine traveled from New York to Waverly for a photo shoot. In 1971, producer-director Russ Meyers announced his plans to film a horror movie, titled *The Eleven*, at the old mansion; it is the story of a ruthless millionaire who is intent on sending eleven people to hell so he can sit at the devil's right hand. Veteran actors John Carradine and Kent Taylor were named to appear in *The Eleven*, which, by all accounts, was never made. In May 1981, *Playboy* magazine photographer Arny Freytag visited Waverly to shoot photographs for the September 1981 pictorial "Girls of the Southeastern Conference." The Snows did not permit any nude photographs to be taken at their home, so Freytag staged a picnic scene at Waverly instead. In 1996, Waverly was featured in an A&E television program titled *America's Castles: The Castles of the Confederacy*, along with the Phelan House in Memphis; the White House of the Confederacy in Westmont, Virginia; and Robert E. Lee's home in Arlington, Virginia. One of the stories in the Waverly segment focused on two notable figures in the history of the Confederacy: Confederate spy Belle Edmonson, who sought refuge in Colonel Young's home, and General Nathan Bedford Forrest, who recuperated from a serious illness in the mansion. The Snow family spent months searching for photographs and letters to be used in the program.

Much of the historic home's media coverage has focused on Waverly's ghost stories. In 1996, Waverly was featured in the Learning Channel program *Hauntings Across America*. This popular show caught the attention of Larry King, who was intrigued by Waverly's haunted history. In 2001, shots from Waverly mansion were featured on the *Larry King Live* show. Many locals hoped that the talk show host's visit to West Point would help put the Golden Triangle on the map.

Even though area residents had been talking about the haunting of Waverly for years, the historic mansion's ghost stories did not become widely known until Kathryn Tucker Windham wrote about them in her book *Thirteen Mississippi Ghosts and Jeffrey* (1974). She begins her account of the haunting of Waverly with a legend that was being passed around West Point and Columbus long before the Snows moved into the house. People who had spent the night in the mansion spoke of hearing the spectral sounds of dancing feet, ethereal music and boisterous laughter. Some visitors to the home claimed to have seen a mosaic of ghostly faces peering out of the floor-length mirror. The story that most people related when asked about Waverly's ghosts involved the spirit of Major John "Jack" Pitchlynn Sr. The orphaned son of an English officer, Pitchlynn was raised by the Choctaws around what is now West Point. Pitchlynn learned the ways of the Choctaws and even married a Choctaw woman. However, he easily adapted to the lifestyle of the whites who were moving into the Golden Triangle. Major Pitchlynn served as an interpreter for the U.S. government after the Revolutionary War. By the time he passed away, Major Pitchlynn had become a very wealthy and influential man. His grave site was a small vacant field near what is now Waverly. In his will, he indicated that he wished to be buried in the Choctaw fashion, with his guns, his boots and his saddle. He also wanted his horse to be killed and placed in the grave with him. Judge Samuel Gholson, overcome with sympathy for the animal, pleaded with Pitchlynn's widow to spare the horse's life. He assured her that the Great Spirit would provide her husband with a fine stallion in the afterlife. Mrs. Pitchlynn placed a brick border around her late husband's grave, which she visited twice a year. The bricks are gone now, but the occupant of the old grave still makes his forceful presence known on moonlit nights when locals hear the faint staccato of hoof beats and catch a glimpse of Major Pitchlynn galloping across the prairie near Waverly on his phantom horse.

The Snows experienced Waverly's haunted history firsthand not long after they moved in. During their first week in the old house, they were awakened in the middle of the night by what sounded like an explosion. They couldn't tell if the explosion occurred inside or outside of the house. Thinking that something terrible had just happened, Donna and Robert turned on the lights and made a thorough search of the house. They were relieved, and a bit mystified, when they discovered that nothing was damaged. A few nights later, the pounding sound of an explosion echoed through the house once again. A second search of the house also yielded no evidence of an explosion. Over the next year, these nocturnal explosive noises continued to interrupt the Snows' sleep. After a few months, though, the family was not particularly alarmed by the strange sound, proving that human beings can become accustomed to almost anything. Someone would say, "There's that noise again!" and then go back to sleep. Over a decade later, Donna said that it "sounded like the noise made by slapping a big board or some other wide, flat object down on the surface of water with great force." She interpreted the noise as evidence that something did not want her and her family living in the mansion. Apparently, the supernatural presences in the house eventually grew accustomed to the Snows living there because they never heard the startling noise again after that first year.

A few months after the noises ceased, Donna made the acquaintance of Waverly's most famous ghost. In an interview given to Kay Hugghins, staff writer for the *Waverly Times Leader* in 1983, Donna said:

> *We had been in the house about two years, all the while working and repairing, when one beautiful spring day about 10:30 in the morning, I was in an upstairs bedroom and heard a sweet little angelic voice right at my feet say,* "Mama, Mama." *There was no warm air, no bright lights or anything* [like that], *and the voice was not in distress or crying. I was so sure that I had heard someone that I even went out on the balcony.*

Donna talked herself into accepting the probability that what she had heard was actually the chattering of a bird, and she went back to her cleaning.

However, this was not her last encounter with the little ghost of Waverly. "The voice began calling to me once a day," Donna said. "She never called to me more than once a day, and she wasn't confined to a particular room or time of day. If the voice had been a grown person's, I would have been frightened, but it was such a sweet little girl's voice that it never occurred to me to be afraid. And if I had ever lost a child, I'm sure that it would have driven me crazy."

Donna continued hearing the little girl's sweet, ghostly voice, and she slowly got used to it, just as she and her family had learned to live with the nightly "booms" during their first year in the house. "It was just a part of our lives," she said. "Then, in the same upstairs bedroom where I had first heard her call to me, an indentation would appear on the bedspread, just as if a young child were sleeping on the bed, in the early afternoon, and it would be gone at night." Determined to solve the mystery of the strange indentations on the bed—or, perhaps, eager to actually see the small specter—Donna and her husband decided to watch the bed. "At the time, we had a teenage son who slept in that bedroom. Well, around four thirty that afternoon, the wrinkles that were in the spread just straightened up. We just couldn't believe it, but there it was, right before our eyes." Donna envisioned a small child who had become tired after playing outside all day climbing up the stairs to her bedroom to take a nap.

The Snow family learned to live with the ghost's afternoon naps as well. In 1974, the ghost made her final attempt to communicate with Donna. She was standing in the kitchen when she heard the tiny voice right next to her. In fact, the voice was so close that Donna half expected the specter to reach up and grab her apron. The tone of her voice had changed as well. "Instead of sweetly calling, the little voice loudly screamed, 'Mama!' about five times. And she was so obviously in distress that I impulsively asked if I could help her. After that day, she never called to me or slept on the bed again. The incident really upset me because I felt as if I knew the child and she was just beyond my reach," Donna said.

Donna was not the only member of the Snow family who has gotten "up close and personal" with their little ghost. Several of the Snow children saw the child while they were growing up in the house. One of the Snows' daughters saw the little girl float up the stairway. "I was more curious than anything when I first saw our ghost," said Cindy Snow Henson, who was five years old when she saw the little spirit.

> One day, I saw this small child dressed in a white linen gown. She was walking along the second-floor balcony. She looked at me, and I looked at her. Then she began to climb the stairs to the third floor. I tried to follow her, but she disappeared. When I asked my mother who the little girl was, she nonchalantly replied, "Oh, that must be our little ghost."

Cindy distinctly recalled that the girl's feet did not make contact with the stairs.

In 1985, Cindy's sister Melanie and a friend made a midnight visit to Waverly. They left their luggage in the library and went to the downstairs powder room to get ready for bed. They were walking up the stairs when, suddenly, they heard a loud banging sound coming from the powder room. They rushed back downstairs, and when they opened the door to

Cindy Snow Henson was five years old when she saw the apparition of a little girl float up the stairs. Photograph taken in 1936. *Courtesy of the Library of Congress.*

the powder room, they were shocked to discover that their makeup bags were on the floor. The bags were open, and the makeup was scattered everywhere. The girls concluded that the childish ghost had decided to play dress-up at their expense.

Those who have seen the ghost describe her as a three-year-old girl with long blond hair. She is usually wearing either a white nightgown or high-collared blue dress. The little girl's afternoon naps still occur, but not very often. The bodily impressions on the bed in what the tour guides call the "Ghost Room" usually appear between 2:00 and 4:00 p.m.

No one knew the identity of the little girl until 1997, when research into the family records of a physician named Dr. Burt revealed her name. In 1862, Dr. Burt left Lowndes County to assist with the fighting at the Battle of Shiloh. While he was away, the older of his two daughters contracted diphtheria. With no slaves to assist her in the care of the child, Mrs. Burt, in desperation, took her two daughters to Waverly. The Youngs did their best to cure the little girl, but she passed away on the third day of her arrival. The next morning, the Burts' four-year-old daughter woke up before anyone else in the house and decided to play on the stairs leading from the second to the third floor. Apparently, she stuck her head through the spindles and was

A little girl who was staying at Waverly during the Civil War is believed to have caught her head between the spindles in the balustrade and broken her neck. *Courtesy Library of Congress.*

unable to extricate herself. By the time Mrs. Burt discovered that the child was no longer in her bed and went searching for her, it was too late. The girl had died of a broken neck while struggling to free herself.

Other ghosts haunt the old mansion, as well. Todd Childs, who was caretaker between 1996 and 1999, was giving a tour one day for seventy-five people. Because the group was so large, he split it into two separate groups. When the tours were over, he ushered the last visitor out of the door and locked it. Todd turned around and was surprised to see a man standing on the second floor with his hands behind his back. His back was turned, and he was staring at the balcony door. Todd shouted up at the man, "I'm sorry, but I thought everyone had gone!" He walked over to the door and unlocked it. "So I waited a minute for him to come back, still believing he was a tourist," Todd said. "These two staircases are the only way down from the upstairs, and he didn't come down either one, so I went up. I thought maybe he'd gone into one of the bedrooms. I searched all four bedrooms and looked down all the balconies. No one could have gotten down without using the stairs."

Todd had another ghostly encounter with the male apparition four years later. When he arrived in the morning, he placed his coat on the sofa. Later in the afternoon, when the temperature dropped, Todd walked through the kitchen and passed through the dining room. "I looked out of the corner of my eye, and there was a man standing right by the door looking into this room," Todd said. "I turned, and just as I looked at him and he looked at me, he turned and walked back toward the staircase. He wasn't out of view the whole time. As he walked out in the hallway, I ran after him, but he wasn't there. He's the only ghost I have seen."

Firsthand accounts suggest that Donna Snow may have become a ghost herself. In the late 1990s, a tour guide named Melissa had just completed her tour and was guiding her group through the first-floor hallway when one of the tourists said there was a redheaded woman sitting on the third-floor stairs smoking a cigarette. From the woman's description of the apparition, Melissa could tell that she had just seen the ghost of Mrs. Snow. As a rule, Mrs. Snow only smoked outside. However, on cold or rainy days, she frequently smoked on the steps leading to the third floor because she believed the smoke would be less noticeable on the first and second floors.

Another female spirit appears only in one of the large mirrors. A docent wearing a nineteenth-century dress was standing in front of a mirror in one of the upstairs bedrooms lacing up her corset. "She said that she was standing in front of one of the mirrors, and behind her in the mirror, she saw

Tour guides and visitors have seen images of faces in the antique mirrors. Photograph taken in 1936. *Courtesy of the Library of Congress.*

a woman come out of the bedroom," Todd said. "She was in an evening gown. When she turned around, the woman was gone." Todd went on to say that he has seen startling images in Waverly's antique mirrors: "A lot of times, you'll catch things out of the corner of your eye. You'll be walking by the mirror, and you'll turn around, and you'll catch little glimpses of things."

Mischievous acts attributable to no specific ghost occasionally disrupt the tranquility of Waverly. Objects turn up missing on a fairly regular basis. In her book *Ghosts! Personal Accounts of Modern Mississippi Hauntings*, Sylvia Booth Hubbard said that one day, Donna Snow's peach pickle spoon disappeared. She searched through the entire kitchen but could not find it anywhere. Knowing the ghost's tendency to hide things, Donna decided to search the whole house. She finally discovered the peach pickle spoon inside a bowl on the top shelf of a display case. In 1999, an employee of Waverly named Carolyn Dickert put her canvas bag in a little nook over by the stove. Todd had to get a haircut, so he placed his keys on the little shelf on the other side of the doorway. "I took a shower, shaved, and my keys were gone!" Todd said. "She had a tour group, and she had not even been in the kitchen." After her tour ended, Carolyn and Todd looked through the entire house. They even searched under the furniture. Unable to think of any other potential hiding place, Tom asked Carolyn to look in her purse. "She dumped her bag on the table, and the only things in her bag were an apple, a sandwich, a Coke in a can and a paperback book. That evening, when she got ready to go home, she looked in her bag and there were my keys. We still don't know how they got there."

Some of the camera crews that have filmed documentaries and television programs at Waverly have accidentally recorded evidence of paranormal activity. Todd Childs recalled one such recording session by the A&E network:

> *While they were filming an interview in the hallway, Robert Snow and I were sitting on the front porch. It was completely quiet inside and outside. No tourists were present at all that day. Right in the middle of the interview, there was this immense crashing sound. Mr. Robert and I ran inside, thinking that something had happened to the equipment. We searched the entire house but couldn't find anything. When we replayed the video, the sound of the crash was on the film.*

Over the years, Todd has heard an assortment of phantom noises, such as the breaking of glass and ghostly voices, but the exploding or crashing sound is the most persistent.

A few years later, another camera crew captured something strange at Waverly. "The camera man was halfway down the yard taking pictures of the front of the house," Todd said. "When the pictures were developed, there was a huge ball of light to the left of the doorway. This was pretty strange because there are no reflective surfaces on the front of the house. The glass panes around the door pane are red, and they don't light."

Most of the docents are not really afraid to work at Waverly because they have gotten used to the ghosts. However, Todd Childs is not comfortable in every room in the house: "I've slept in every other room in the house and have even stayed here alone for days at a time, but I will not stay in the room to the left of the Ghost Room. I can't explain it. I get a very uneasy feeling whenever I go in there."

BIBLIOGRAPHY

Books

Barfoot, Daniel. *Haunted Halls of Ivy: Ghosts of Southern Colleges and Universities.* Winston-Salem, NC: John F. Blair, 2004.

Beck, Brandon H. *The Battle of Okolona: Defending the Mississippi Prairie.* Charleston, SC: The History Press, 2009.

Brown, Alan. *Haunted Places in the American South.* Jackson: University Press of Mississippi, 2002.

Brunvand, Jan Howard. *The Choking Doberman and Other "New" Urban Legends.* New York: W.W. Norton & Company, 1984.

Cheung, Theresa. *Element Encyclopedia of Ghosts and Hauntings: The Ultimate A–Z of Spirits, Mysteries and the Paranormal.* New York: Harper-Element, 2009.

Cobb, Joseph B. *Mississippi Scenes; or, Sketches of Southern and Western Life and Adventure, Humorous, Satirical, and Descriptive, Including the Legend of Black Creek.* Philadelphia: Hart, 1851.

Escott, Paul. "The Art and Science of Reading WPA Slave Narratives." In *The Slave's Narrative*, edited by Charles T. Davis and Henry Louis Gates. New York: Oxford University Press, 1985.

Higginbotham, Sylvia. *Reflections: Homes and History of Columbus, Mississippi.* Louisville, KY: Everbest Publishing, 2001.

Kempe, Helen Kerr. *Old Homes of Mississippi.* Vol. 2, *Columbus and the North.* Gretna, LA: Pelican Publishing Company, 1977.

Lloyd, James B. *Lives of Mississippi Authors, 1817–1967.* Jackson: University Press of Mississippi, 2009.

Neilson, Sarah. *Old Homes and Scenes of Columbus and Lowndes County*. Columbus: Association for the Preservation of Columbus and Lowndes County Antiquities, 1965.

Pascoe, Jill. *Mississippi's Haunted Mansions*. Gilbert, AZ: Irongate Press, 2012.

Scott, Michael, Norman Scott and Beth Scott. *Haunted America*. New York: Tor Books, 1994.

Vance, Mona. *Images of America: Columbus*. Charleston, SC: Arcadia Publishing, 2011.

Waters, Andrew, ed. *"Prayin' to Be Set Free": Personal Accounts of Slavery in Mississippi*. Winston-Salem, NC: John F. Blair, Publisher, 2002.

Windham, Kathryn Tucker. *13 Mississippi Ghosts and Jeffrey*. Tuscaloosa: University of Alabama Press, 1974.

ARTICLES

Ancestry.com. "Lowndes County, Mississippi: Largest Slaveholders from 1860 Census Schedules and Surname Matches for African Americans on 1870 Census." http://frepagesgenealogy/rootswebancestry.com/~ajac/mslowndes.htmAnderson.

Anderson, Hilton. "A Southern 'Sleepy Hollow.'" *Mississippi Folklore Register* 3 (n.d.): 85–88.

Blogspot. "Three-Legged Lady Road." http://paranormalstories.comblogspot.com/2011/03/three-legged-lady-road.html.

Exploresouthernhistory.com. "Birthplace of Tennessee Williams. http://www.exploresouthernhistory.com/columbusms.html.

———. "Home of Gen. Stephen D. Lee—Columbus, Mississippi. http://www.exploresouthernhistory.com/stephendlee.html.

FamilySearch. "Jackson's Military Road." https://familysearch.org/wiki/en/Jack.

Growth Alliance. "History of West Point and other facts." http://wpnet.prgomdes/[j[vosotprspir_history.

HauntedHouses.com. "Five Antebellum Mansions." http://hauntedhouses.com/states/ms/antebellum_mansions.htm.

Hauntspot.com. "Railroad Tracks on Armstrong Road." http://www.hauntspot.com/haunt/usa/mississippi/railroad-tracks-on-armstrong-road.shtml.

Lowndes, Mississippi Genealogy & History Network. "Friendship Cemetery." http://lowndes.msghn.org/Friendship/Friendship.shtml.

Mississippi State University. "George Hall." http://map.msstate.edu/map/accessible.php?id-233.

———. "Historical Buildings—Mississippi State University Libraries." www.lib.msstate.edu/exhibits/msu-buildings.

————. "Montgomery Hall." http://map.msstate.edu/map/assessible. php?id-233.

————."Our History." www.muw.edu.

————. "University History." www.msstate.edu/about/history.

MSGenWeb Slave Narrative Project. "Jerry Eubanks Age 91 Years." http://msgw.org/slaves/eubanks-xslave.htm.

Onlyinyourstate. "These 9 Haunted Hotels in Mississippi Will Make Your State a Nightmare." www.onlyinourstate.com>haunted-ms.

Paranormal & Ghost Society. "Ghost Hunters Converging on Downtown's Princess." https://groups.yahoo.com/groups/ParanormalGhostSociety/conversations/messages/54444.

Southern Spirit Guide. "Haunted Columbus, Mississippi." http://southernspiritguide.blogspot.com/2010/haunted-columbus-mississippi.html.

Stephen D. Lee Home & Museum. "History." http: www.leehomemuseum.com/history.html.

Thecityofcolumbus.ms. "History of Columbus." http://www.thecityofcolumbus.ms.gov/Pages/History.aspx.

Wikimedia.org. Mississippi Landmark Gregg-Hamilton. Commons. m.wikimedia.org>wiki.

Wikipedia. "Columbus Mississippi." https://en.wikipedia.org/wiki/Columbus,_Mississippi.

————. "Golden Triangle (Mississippi)." https://en.wikipedia.org/wiki/Golden_Triangle_(Mississippi).

————. "Jackson's Military Road. https://en.wikipedia.org/wiki/Jackson527s_Military_Road.

————. "West Point, Mississippi." https//en.wikpedia.org/wiki/Waverly_(West_Point_Missisippi).

NEWSPAPERS

Atkinson, Hal. "Stately Waverly Mansion." *Daily-Times Leader*, August 10, 1966.

Brigham, Allegra. "Honey Bees Swarm at Waverly as Snows' Restoration Continues." *Commercial Dispatch*, April 18, 1976.

Brooks, Pat. "Belter Antiques to Be a Feature in Columbus Pilgrimage Tour." *Aberdeen (MS) Examiner*, April 4, 1968.

————. "Valentine Ghosts Visits 'Sticks.'" *Commercial Dispatch*, February 22 1968.

Browning, William. "With Halloween upon Us, a Look at Area Hauntings." *Commercial Dispatch*, October 28, 2008.

Brumfield, Carroll. "Mansion to Be Site of Hollywood Film." *Memphis Commercial Appeal*, October 23, 1971.

Clark, Dot. "Waverly Mansion Is Cited." *Commercial Dispatch*, December 15, 1968.

Commercial Appeal. "Waverly Mansion Is Home for 25 Species of Pheasant." July 17, 1965.

Commercial Dispatch. "Donna and Robert Snow Restore Waverly's Glory." March 30, 1986.

———. "Phantom-Bellum Homes." October 27, 1996.

———. "The Princess Theater Story." May 26, 1996.

Connell, Moody, and Conswella Bennett. "Waverly Mansion Focus of *Larry King Live* Show." *Commercial Dispatch*, April 3, 2001.

Cook, K.W. "The Rise of the House of Waverly." *Commercial Appeal*, January 4, 1969.

Cortese, James. "Ghost of Aged House 'Carves' Out a Living." *Commercial Appeal*, n.d.

Cress, Dacia. "Waverly Mansion Welcomes Film Crews." *Starkville Daily News*, July 29, 1996.

Descent, Earl. "Aging Princess May Get Back on Her Feet Thanks to Doctor." *Commercial Dispatch*, January 12, 2006.

Fleming, Anne. "Waverly, Abandoned for Half a Century, Is Now in the Process of Loving Restoration." *Clarksdale Press Register*, October 21, 1965.

Harper, Phyllis, and Leslie Harper. "Mansion Lost for Half Century: Restored Waverly." *Daily Journal*, March 30, 1976.

Henry, Margaret. "Old Clock Tower Bell Will Peal as MUW Rings in the Bicentennial." *Commercial Dispatch*, July 2, 1976.

Hugghins, Kay. "Waverly's Little Girl Ghost Hasn't Shown Up in Eight Years Now." *Times Leader*, October 26, 1983.

James, Russell. "Hunting for Haunts—Stories abound about Ghosts of Columbus." *Commercial Dispatch*, October 5, 2003.

Jones, Emily. "Things That Go Bump in the Night." *Starkville Daily News*, October 29, 2006.

Monteith, Gene. "Waverly Mansion May Get Exposure in *Playboy*—but SEC Coeds Won't." *Clarion-Ledger*, April 29, 1981.

———. "Waverly Owners Await Mansion Ghost's Return." *Clarion-Ledger*, April 13, 1980.

Murray, Danny. "Serenity of Past to Be Broken at Waverly for Movie Production." *Daily Journal*, April 21, 1972.

Neyman, Martha. "Local Apparitions Plentiful." *Commercial Dispatch*, April 12, 1998.

Novet, Jordan. "Ghosts of the Friendly City." *Commercial Dispatch*, July 3, 2008.

Poag, Aliene. "Past Remains Preserved at the Princess." *Commercial Dispatch*, November 12, 1989.

Ricks, Kay. "Waverly Pictured Perfectly." *Times Leader*, October 19, 1984.

Robinson, J.W. "Waverly Mansion: Restored Beauty and History, Too." *Times Leader*, June 6, 1979.

Sisson, Carmen. "Fall Tour of Homes Illustrates Diversity of Architectural Styles." *Commercial Dispatch*, October 6, 2011.

Thompson, Ray M. "Historic Waverly." *Daily Herald*, May 10, 1962.

Waide, Jacque. "When Things Go Bump in the Night." *Commercial Dispatch*, October 30, 1988.

Ward, Rufus. "Friendship Cemetery, a Walk Through History." *Commercial Dispatch*, September 26, 2015.

———. "The Legend of Black Creek." *Starkville Dispatch*, October 24, 2010.

Weneth, George. "Antebellum Home Gets Face-Lift." *Mobile Press Register*, August 24, 1980.

Wilson, Clyude Hill. "Former Residents of Gregg-Hamilton Recall Sound of Unusual Footsteps in the Night." *Aberdeen Examiner*, February 21, 1995.

PAMPHLETS

Richardson, Emma, Pat Ross, Tom Lewis and Mary Bess Paluzzi. *Friendship Cemetery Brochure*. Columbus: City of Columbus and the Mississippi School for Mathematics and Science, n.d.

Waverly Plantation and Carl Butler. *Memorial to Anti-Bellum Elegance*. September 1999.

INTERVIEWS

Butler, Dixie. January 30, 2004.
Carradine, Sid. December 14, 2015.
Childs, Todd. January 26, 2001.
Herriott, Gloria. January 27, 2016.
Herriott, Maurice. February 13, 2016.
Holcomb, Misty. December 23, 2000.
Pieschel, Bridget. February 4, 2004.
Reynolds, Kenny. March 3, 2005.

MISCELLANEOUS

Bullock, Charles, and Jan Bullock. "Ole Magnolia History." N.d.

Burns, Carolyn J. "A Tour of the Ghosts of Columbus." N.d.

United States Department of the Interior National Park Service. National Register of Historic Places Registration Form. "William E. Ervin House." October 19, 1989.

ABOUT THE AUTHOR

D r. Alan Brown has been a professor of English at the University of West Alabama since 1986. For the past few years, Dr. Brown's interest in southern folklore has manifested itself in several collections of southern ghost stories, including *The Face in the Window and Other Alabama Ghostlore* (1996); *Shadows and Cypress* (2000); *Haunted Places in the American South* (2002); *Stories from the Haunted South* (2004); *Ghost Hunters of the South* (2006); *Haunted Georgia* (2007); *Haunted Texas* (2008); *Ghost Hunters of New England* (2008); *Haunted Tennessee* (2008); *Haunted Kentucky* (2009); *Haunted Birmingham* (2009); *Haunted Vicksburg* (2010); *Haunted Natchez* (2010); *Haunted Meridian, Mississippi* (2011); *Ghosts along the Mississippi River* (2011); *The Big Book of Texas Ghost Stories* (2010); and *Ghosts along Florida's Gulf Coast* (2015). He has also investigated a number of haunted sites, including the Artist's House in Key West, Florida; Miss Molly's Bed and Breakfast in Fort Worth, Texas; King's Tavern in Natchez, Mississippi; and the Waverly Hills Tuberculosis Sanatorium in Louisville, Kentucky.

CPSIA information can be obtained
at www.ICGtesting.com
Printed in the USA
LVHW021103210720
661194LV00020B/826